MEMORIES OF MY FATHER, JOYCE KILMER

Kenton Kilmer

KENTON KILMER

JOYCE KILMER CENTENNIAL COMMISSION, INC.

B-Kil

ACKNOWLEDGEMENT IS MADE TO
JOHNSON & JOHNSON
FOR THEIR CONTRIBUTION TOWARD
THE DISTRIBUTION OF THIS NEW BOOK
TO NEW JERSEY SCHOOL LIBRARIES.

ACKNOWLEDGEMENT IS ALSO MADE TO
DOUBLEDAY OF NEW YORK
FOR PERMISSION TO USE SOME OF
JOYCE KILMER AND ALINE KILMER POEMS,
AND TO JERRY VOGEL MUSIC COMPANY, INC. OF NEW YORK
FOR PERMISSION TO USE *TREES*.

Published by the
Joyce Kilmer Centennial Commission, Inc.
Joyce Kilmer Birthplace
17 Joyce Kilmer Avenue
New Brunswick, N.J. 08901-2507
(908) 572-0524

ISBN 0-9637524-0-5

First Edition

Trees

I think that I shall never see
A poem lovely as a tree,

A tree whose hungry mouth is prest
Against the earth's sweet flowing breast;

A tree that looks at god all day
And lifts her leafy arms to pray;

A tree that may in Summer wear
A nest of robins in her hair;

Upon whose bosom snow has lain;
Who intimately lives with rain

Poems are made by fools like me
But only God can make a tree.

Joyce Kilmer

THIS BOOK HAS BEEN PRINTED ON RECYCLED PAPER BECAUSE
"...ONLY GOD CAN MAKE A TREE."

MEMORIES OF MY FATHER, JOYCE KILMER

TABLE OF CONTENTS

Introduction 1
1. Celebrating Individuals, Enjoying Differences.....................3
    Folly (For A.K.K.), by Joyce Kilmer 6
    Delicatessen, by J.K. 7
    Dave Lilly, by J.K. 10
    St. Alexis, Patron of Beggars, by J.K. 12
    Martin, by J.K. 14
    Servant Girl and Grocer's Boy, by J.K. 16
    Roofs, by J.K...17
2. Delight in Food 18
3. Tracing Relationships and Friendships through Time 22
    My Mirror, by Aline Kilmer 27
    Tribute, by A.K. 28
    Against the Wall, by A.K...29
    For the Birthday of a Middle-Aged Child, by A.K........30
    Experience, by A.K. 31
    Candles That Burn, by A.K. 32
    A Wind in the Night, by A.K. 33
    Atonement, by A.K..34
    After Grieving, by A.K. 35
    I Shall Not Be Afraid, by A.K. 36
4. Reading and Writing and Poem Reciting............................37
    In Memory, by J.K. 40
    As Winds That Blow Against a Star
    (For Aline), by J.K. 42
    Song, by A.K. 43
    The Proud Poet (For Shaemas O'Sheel)
    (Excerpt), by J.K. 44
    Father Gerard Hopkins, S.J., by J.K.........................45
    In Memory of Rupert Brooke, by J.K.........................46
    Moonlight, by A.K..47
5. Poetry: Fun and Fury..48
    To a Young Poet Who Killed Himself, by J.K. 50
6. Fun With Books 51
    The Gift, by A.K...56
    Love's Lantern (For Aline), by J.K. 57
    Vision (For Aline), by J.K. 58
    Ptolemaic, by A.K...59
    Favete Linguis, by A.K. 60

7. Disappointments—and a Glad Surprise 61
    Pennies, by J.K. 63
8. The Time I Froze to Death! (Well, Almost).......................64
    The Snowman in the Yard
    (For Thomas Augustine Daly), by J.K. 66
9. Jokes and Play 68
    Main Street, by J.K. 71
10. My First—and Last—Lie 72
11. Themes of Poetry and Life 74
    Apology (For Eleanor Rogers Cox) (Excerpt), by J.K. ...78
    Vigils, by A.K..79
    The Poor King's Daughter, by A.K. 80
    Citizen of the World, by J.K. 81
    A Blue Valentine (For Aline), by J.K. 82
    Roses, by J.K..84
    The Singing Girl, by J.K. 85
    Easter, by J.K. 86
12. Our Mahwah Yard and Neighborhood 87
    The House with Nobody In It, by J.K........................90
    Trees (For Mrs. Henry Mills Alden), by J.K. 92
    Shadows and Light, by Kenton Kilmer 93
    The Twelve-Forty-Five, by J.K. 94
13. Religious Principles and Teaching Ways........................79
    The Rosary, by J.K. 99
    Sanctuary, by A.K. 100
    One Shall Be Taken and the Other Left, by A.K. 101
    If I Had Loved You More, by A.K. 102
14. Our Irish and Irish-American Friends and Relations 103
    Gates and Doors, by J.K. 114
    The Fourth Shepherd (For Thomas Walsh), by J.K.....116
15. The Croix de Guerre 118
    The White Ships and the Red, by J.K. 121
    Kings, by J.K. 124
    Rouge Bouquet, by J.K. 125
    The Peacemaker, by J.K. 127
    Prayer of a Soldier, by J.K. 128
    Memorial Day, by J.K..129
16. Joyce Kilmer's letters to his mother,
    Annie Kilburn Kilmer......................................153-261
    Notes...262-270

PAGE	**LIST OF ILLUSTRATIONS**
130	JOYCE KILMER BIRTHPLACE HOUSE—17 CODWISE (NAMED JOYCE KILMER) AVENUE.
131	JOYCE KILMER AGED BETWEEN FIVE & SIX MONTHS; 2 YEARS OLD.
132	JOYCE KILMER 5 YEARS OLD.
133	VALENTINE TO HIS MOTHER; RUTGERS PREPARATORY REPORT CARD.
134	RUTGERS PREPARATORY SCHOOL, 1901.
135	ALINE MURRAY (KILMER), RUTGERS PREPARATORY SCHOOL, 1906.
136	JOYCE KILMER IS THE CHARACTER SIDNEY CARLTON, WITH HIS MOTHER, 1907.
137	FREDERICK BARNETT KILMER, VICE PRESIDENT, R & D, AT JOHNSON & JOHNSON.
138	JOYCE KILMER, B.A. FROM COLUMBIA UNIVERSITY, 1908.
139	JOYCE KILMER (COLUMBIA, 1908) WITH HIS MOTHER.
140	1963 PHOTOGRAPH OF NEW BRUNSWICK TREE BY LELAND A. COOK.
141	JOYCE KILMER AND HIS MOTHER ON A RETURN TRIP FROM EUROPE (1914).
142	JOYCE KILMER & A GROUP TO FIGHT A MAHWAH, N.J. BRUSH FIRE, 1916.
143	ANNIE KILBURN KILMER, MOTHER OF JOYCE KILMER, TAKEN AT JOYCE'S REQUEST.
144	PRIVATE JOYCE KILMER, JUST AFTER HIS TRANSFER TO THE 165TH (69TH) REGIMENT.
145	POST CARD FROM FRANCE, AND SGT. JOYCE KILMER SENT FROM FRANCE (MAY, 1918).
146	ALINE KILMER, 1919.
147	ROSE KILBURN KILMER (ROSAMONDE), 1912-1917.
148	ALINE KILMER & CHILDREN IN LARCHMONT, NEW YORK, 1920.
149	KENTON KILMER, 1920.
150	PORTRAIT OF JOYCE KILMER (C)1981, BY MIRIAM A. KILMER, GRANDDAUGHTER.
151	KENTON KILMER, 1920, (C)1992 BY MIRIAM A. KILMER.
152	HIGHLAND PARK HOTEL, 75 YEARS AGO, & DOUGHBOY STATUE & TREE STUMP.

INTRODUCTION

On Armistice Day, 1918, Larchmont was bright with flapping flags, and loud with shouts and cheers, laughter and joyous noise. The war was over, and everyone in town rejoicing. When I went home from school, through this loud tumult, I found my mother crying. I asked her (and I don't know how I could have been so obtuse) why she was crying when people all around were happy that the war was over. She told me that others were happy because their sons, or husbands, or fathers, were out of great danger and would soon be coming home, but that her dear husband, my father, had been killed, and we would never see him again. I cried with her.

Long afterward, in the autumn of 1941, in the course of Mother's prolonged death of cancer, she suddenly roused from sleep or coma, and cried out in a tone of unmistakable glad recognition, "Joyce!" I was with her then, waiting and giving what help I could through the long weeks of her dying, and I am happy to feel that she did, then, see her dear husband again.

In the course of this series of reminiscences, I am mentioning various members of the family from time to time, and I think it would be helpful to the reader for me to identify them here.

Dad's father, Dr. Frederick Barnett Kilmer, generally known more shortly as Dr. Fred B. Kilmer, was one of the founders, and long-time chief chemist, of Johnson & Johnson. I knew him as Grandad, probably using that form of the title because Dad called him "Dad." Dad's mother, Annie Kilburn Kilmer, was proud of her English heritage, as a descendant of Baron Kilburn, one of the signers of Magna Carta. I knew her as Granny, probably her own choice of title. They had four children, two of whom died in infancy. Dad's elder brother, Anda, who had worked in the advertising department of Johnson & Johnson, had died before I was born. His family doesn't enter into these reminiscences, though his daughter Eleanor Kilmer Sceva was closely associated with us, and even lived with us for some periods.

Mother's father, Kenton C. Murray, editor of the Norfolk *Landmark*, had died in 1895. His widow, Ada Foster Murray,

1

married Henry Mills Alden, editor of *Harper's Magazine*, about 1900. The Murray children were six, one of whom died as a young child. The ones I knew best were my mother's elder sister, Ada Murray Clarke, and her younger sister, Constance Murray Greene. Ada Clarke is mentioned in a letter from Sarah Coerr, in Chapter 3, and Constance in a discussion of family theatricals in the New Brunswick household, in Chapter 6. Ada Alden was a poet of some distinction, and a talented story-teller. I knew her as Gran, since when I came along she had already been so christened by my elder cousins. I knew Henry Mills Alden as Grandaddy, probably because his three daughters (by his first wife) and his step-children, all called him Daddy.

When I was very young, as I learned later from Mother, I called my parents by the names I heard them call each other—in the *way* I heard them. Dad was "Jyce," and Mother was "Ailie." When Rose, my sister, born in 1912, was nursing, my mother told me, I cried out in alarm: "Jyce, Jyce, the new baby is eating Ailie!" Rose died in September, 1917, shortly before Dad's regiment sailed for France, and Christopher was born later that same month. Deborah was born in November, 1914, and is now living as Sister M. Michael Kilmer, OSB. Michael was born in February, 1916, and died in 1927.

Christopher lived to serve, during World War II, in Dad's Regiment, married and had four children, and died in 1984. Each year, I circulate among the family a list of our descendants, including their spouses, stepchildren, and adopted children. The total now runs to seventy-four people in some way descended from Joyce and Aline Kilmer. We may all take pride in that heritage, and try to be worthy of it.

1. CELEBRATING INDIVIDUALS, ENJOYING DIFFERENCES

In the spring of 1991, I was gratified to learn of the honor paid to my father's memory at Paul Robeson High School, in New Brunswick. I particularly treasure the linking of my Dad's name with that of Paul Robeson because of the magnificent rendering of "Trees" by Robeson, on a phonograph record, as well as frequently in concerts. I like to remember, also, a small but courageous gesture on the part of my grandmother. Annie Kilburn Kilmer, when Robeson was a Rutgers student. My mother told me of it, with a gleam of pride in her eyes, and evident whole-hearted approval. It was customary, in those days, for a student outstanding in his studies, *or* notably successful in student theatrical or musical performances, *or* a star performer in football or other sports, to be given social recognition by the ladies at a tea. Paul Robeson, if my mother's opinions and my memory are correct, qualified on all counts, but was being ignored because of his color. Granny was filled with righteous wrath about this, but took an eminently peaceful way of combating this discrimination. She found a convenient date for Paul Robeson, and duly sent out the formal invitations for the ladies to meet him. Then she whirled in, with her customary energy, and made sure of plenty of the home-made bread for which her household was noted, home-made preserves, cake, cookies, and I don't know what other goodies. She and her cook, Nettie or Mary Armstrong, or others whose names I don't remember, were always a formidable team in preparing festivities. You can well imagine, too, with what enthusiasm a black cook must have entered into this project!

Like many of my memories, this one is only peripherally connected with Dad, but I know his spirit was with his mother all the way in this endeavor to give Paul Robeson his due honor. In his patriotism, as well as in his religion, Dad was fervently inclusive. His scorn was reserved for those who scorned others, whether for cultural or financial or racial differences. He was exuberantly appreciative of differences, relishing typical English cooking, for example, as shown so often in his advice to his mother on what to eat in London; hurraying for the gypsy because, "He never goes a-wandering,

3

but he takes his home along"; and for Dave Lilly because "He was shiftless and good-for-nothing, but he certainly could fish." Dad became a socialist, I am sure, because he thought socialism embodied his enthusiasm for down-trodden and unfortunate individuals—but he abandoned socialism, I am also sure, because he perceived that its concern was a cold and philosophical interest in the welfare of the masses, and tended to ignore individuals, families, and emotional relationships.

Consistently, in his poetry, my father celebrates the individual person, whether man, woman, or child, with emphasis on those who may, for any reason, be looked down upon by others. His fullest statement of this feeling is in the conclusion of "Delicatessen":

> This man has home and child and wife
> And battle set for every day.
> This man has God and love and life;
> These stand, all else shall pass away.
>
> O Carpenter of Nazareth,
> Whose mother was a village maid,
> Shall we, Thy children, blow our breath
> In scorn on any humble trade?
>
> Have pity on our foolishness
> And give us eyes, that we may see
> Beneath the shopman's clumsy dress
> The splendour of humanity!

My father and my mother, and their parents before them, were consistent in teaching that full courtesy and respect were due to each individual, and that the right to such treatment could be forfeited only by the deliberate action of that individual. But this was not, for them, merely a lesson to be learned by rote. Rather, it was a joy to be relished, to note and appreciate the individuality, and the heritage, of each person we might come to know. I felt, therefore, that my father's spirit was with me when I formed, out of poems published in *The Washington Post* while I was poetry editor, the anthology called *This Is My America*. Taking Lieutenant-Colonel William A. Brewer's prose poem of that title as a sort of backbone, I expanded each section of it by adding distinct poems akin to the theme of that section. In the conclusion of

4

my foreword, I briefly stated the theme of the book: "At any time...I think it is good for us to have an emotional, as well as intellectual, realization of the grandeur of the land in which we live, and of the contribution made to that grandeur by the magnificent differences, both in the land itself and in the people who inhabit it. Limestone and coal, desert and meadow, Nordic and Negro, this is my America."

I treasure the memory of the comment my father's friend and biographer made on this book, when I had sent him a copy. Robert Cortes Holliday wrote: "You have deserved well of the Republic." I feel confident that Dad would have agreed.

FOLLY

(For A.K.K.)

What distant mountains thrill and glow
    Beneath our Lady Folly's tread?
Why has she left us, wise in woe.
    Shrewd, practical, uncomforted?
We cannot love or dream or sing.
    We are too cynical to pray,
There is no joy in anything
    Since Lady Folly went away.

Many a knight and gentle maid,
    Whose glory shines from years gone by,
Through ignorance was unafraid
    And as a fool knew how to die.
Saint Folly rode beside Jehanne
    And broke the ranks of Hell with her,
And Folly's smile shone brightly on
    Christ's plaything, Brother Juniper.

Our minds are troubled and defiled
    By study in a weary school.
O for the folly of the child!
    The ready courage of the fool!
Lord, crush our knowledge utterly
    And make us humble, simple men;
And cleansed of wisdom, let us see
    Our Lady Folly's face again.

—Joyce Kilmer

DELICATESSEN

Why is that wanton gossip Fame
    So dumb about this man's affairs?
Why do we twitter at his name
    Who come to buy his curious wares?

Here is a shop of wonderment.
    From every land has come a prize;
Rich spices from the Orient,
    And fruit that knew Italian skies,

And figs that ripened by the sea
    In Smyrna, nuts from hot Brazil,
Strange pungent meats from Germany,
    And currants from a Grecian hill.

He is the lord of goodly things
    That make the poor man's table gay,
Yet of his worth no minstrel sings,
    And on his tomb there is no bay.

Perhaps he lives and dies unpraised
    This trafficker in humble sweets,
Because his little shops are raised
    By thousands in the city streets.

Yet stars in greater numbers shine,
    And violets in millions grow,
And they in many a golden line
    Are sung, as every child must know.

Perhaps Fame thinks his worried eyes,
    His wrinkled, shrewd, pathetic face,
His shop, and all he sells and buys
    Are desperately commonplace.

Well, it is true he has no sword
    To dangle at his booted knees.
He leans across a slab of board,
    And draws his knife and slices cheese.

He never heard of chivalry,
    He longs for no heroic times;
He thinks of pickles, olives, tea,
    And dollars, nickels, cents and dimes.

His world has narrow walls, it seems,
    By counters is his soul confined;
His wares are all his hopes and dreams,
    They are the fabric of his mind.

Yet—in a room above the store
    There is a woman—and a child
Pattered just now across the floor;
    The shopman looked at him and smiled.

For, once he thrilled with high romance
    And turned to love his eager voice.
Like any cavalier of France
    He wooed the maiden of his choice.

And now deep in his weary heart
    Are sacred flames that whitely burn.
He has of Heaven's grace a part
    Who loves, who is beloved in turn.

And when the long day's work is done,
    (How slow the leaden minutes ran!)
Home, with his wife and little son,
    He is no huckster, but a man!

And there are those who grasp his hand,
    Who drink with him and wish him well.
O in no drear and lonely land
    Shall he who honours friendship dwell.

And in his little shop, who knows
    What bitter games of war are played?
Why, daily on each corner grows
    A foe to rob him of his trade.

He fights, and for his fireside's sake;
    He fights for clothing and for bread;
The lances of his foemen make
    A steely halo round his head.

He decks his window artfully,
    He haggles over paltry sums.
In this strange field his war must be
    And by such blows his triumph comes.

What if no trumpet sounds to call
    His arméd legions to his side?
What if to no ancestral hall
    He comes in all a victor's pride?

The scene shall never fit the deed.
    Grotesquely wonders come to pass.
The fool shall mount an Arab steed
    And Jesus ride upon an ass.

This man has home and child and wife
    And battle set for every day.
This man has God and love and life;
    These stand—all else shall pass away.

O Carpenter of Nazareth,
    Whose mother was a village maid,
Shall we, Thy children, blow our breath
    In scorn on any humble trade?

Have pity on our foolishness
    And give us eyes, that we may see
Beneath the shopman's clumsy dress
    The splendour of humanity!

                    —Joyce Kilmer

DAVE LILLY

There's a brook on the side of Greylock that used to be full of
    trout,
But there's nothing there now but minnows, they say it is all
    fished out.
I fished there many a Summer day some twenty years ago,
And I never quit without getting a mess of a dozen or so.

There was a man, Dave Lilly, who lived on the North Adams
    road,
And he spent all his time fishing, while his neighbors reaped
    and sowed.
He was the luckiest fishman in the Berkshire Hills, I think,
And when he didn't go fishing he'd sit in the tavern and drink.

Well, Dave is dead and buried and nobody cares very much,
They have no use in Greylock for drunkards and loafers and
    such.
But I always liked Dave Lilly, he was pleasant as you could
    wish;
He was shiftless and good-for-nothing, but he certainly could
    fish.

The other night I was walking up the hill from Williamstown
And I came to the brook I mentioned, and I stopped on the
    bridge and sat down.
I looked at the blackened water with its little flecks of white
And I heard it ripple and whisper in the still of the Summer
    night.

And after I'd been there a minute it seemed to me I could feel
The presence of someone near me, and I heard the hum of a
    reel.
And the water was churned and broken, and something was
    brought to land
By a twist and flirt of a shadowy rod in a deft and shadowy
    hand.

I scrambled down to the brookside and hunted all about;
There wasn't a sign of a fisherman; there wasn't a sign of a
 trout.
But I heard somebody chuckle behind the hollow oak
And I got a whiff of tobacco like Lilly used to smoke.

It's fifteen years, they tell me, since anyone fished that brook;
And there's nothing in it but minnows that nibble the bait off
 your hook.
But before the sun has risen and after the moon has set
I know that it's full of ghostly trout for Lilly's ghost to get.

I guess I'll go to the tavern and get a bottle of rye
And leave it down by the hollow oak, where Lilly's ghost went
 by.
I meant to go up on the hillside and try to find his grave
And put some flowers on it—but this will be better for Dave.

—Joyce Kilmer

ST. ALEXIS

Patron of Beggars

We who beg for bread as we daily tread
    Country lane and city street,
Let us kneel and pray on the broad highway
    To the saint with the vagrant feet.
Our altar light is a buttercup bright,
    And our shrine is a bank of sod,
But still we share St. Alexis' care,
    The Vagabond of God.

They gave him a home in purple Rome
    And a princess for his bride,
But he rowed away on his wedding day
    Down the Tiber's rushing tide.
And he came to land on the Asian strand
    Where the heathen people dwell;
As a beggar he strayed and he preached and prayed
    And he saved their souls from hell.

Bowed with years and pain he came back again
    To his father's dwelling place.
There was none to see who this tramp might be,
    For they knew not his bearded face.
But his father said, "Give him drink and bread
    And a couch underneath the stair."
So Alexis crept to his hole and slept.
    But he might not linger there.

For when night came down on the seven hilled town,
    And the emperor hurried in,
Saying, "Lo, I hear that a saint is near
    Who will cleanse us of our sin,"
Then they looked in vain where the saint had lain,
    For his soul had fled afar,
From his fleshly home he had gone to roam
    Where the gold-paved highways are.

We who beg for bread as we daily tread
    Country lane and city street,
Let us kneel and pray on the broad highway
    To the saint with the vagrant feet.
Our altar light is a buttercup bright,
    And our shrine is a bank of sod,
But still we share St. Alexis' care,
    The Vagabond of God!

—Joyce Kilmer

MARTIN

When I am tired of earnest men,
    Intense and keen and sharp and clever,
Pursuing fame with brush or pen,
    Or counting metal disks forever,
Then from the halls of Shadowland,
    Beyond the trackless purple sea,
Old Martin's ghost comes back to stand
    Beside my desk and talk to me.

Still on his delicate pale face
    A quizzical thin smile is showing,
His cheeks are wrinkled like fine lace,
    His kind blue eyes are gay and glowing.
He wears a brilliant-hued cravat,
    A suit to match his soft grey hair,
A rakish stick, a knowing hat,
    A manner blithe and debonair.

How good that he who always knew
    That being lovely was a duty,
Should have gold halls to wander through
    And should himself inhabit beauty.
How like his old unselfish way
    To leave those halls of splendid mirth
And comfort those condemned to stay
    Upon the dull and sombre earth.

Some people ask: "What cruel chance
    Made Martin's life so sad a story?"
Martin? Why, he exhaled romance,
    And wore an overcoat of glory.
A fleck of sunlight in the street,
    A horse, a book, a girl who smiled,
Such visions made each moment sweet
    For this receptive ancient child.

14

Because it was old Martin's lot
    To be, not make, a decoration,
Shall we then scorn him, having not
    His genius of appreciation?
Rich joy and love he got and gave;
    His heart was merry as his dress;
Pile laurel leaves upon his grave
    Who did not gain, but was, success!

—Joyce Kilmer

SERVANT GIRL AND GROCER'S BOY

Her lips' remark was: "Oh, you kid!"
Her soul spoke thus (I know it did):

"O king of realms of endless joy,
My own, my golden grocer's boy,

I am a princess forced to dwell
Within a lonely kitchen cell,

While you go dashing through the land
With loveliness on every hand.

Your whistle strikes my eager ears
Like music of the choiring spheres.

The mighty earth grows faint and reels
Beneath your thundering wagon wheels.

How keenly, perilously sweet
To cling upon that swaying seat!

How happy she who by your side
May share the splendours of that ride!

Ah, if you will not take my hand
And bear me off across the land,

Then, traveller from Arcady,
Remain awhile and comfort me.

What other maiden can you find
So young and delicate and kind?"

Her lips' remark was: "Oh, you kid!"
Her soul spoke thus (I know it did).

—Joyce Kilmer

16

ROOFS

The road is wide and the stars are out and the breath of the
    night is sweet,
And this is the time when wanderlust should seize upon my
    feet.
But I'm glad to turn from the open road and the starlight on
    my face,
And to leave the splendour of out-of-doors for a human
    dwelling-place.

I never have seen a vagabond who really liked to roam
All up and down the streets of the world and not to have a
    home;
The tramp who slept in your barn last night and left at break
    of day
Will wander only until he finds another place to stay.

A gypsy-man will sleep in his cart with canvas overhead;
Or else he'll go into his tent when it is time for bed.
He'll sit on the grass and take his ease so long as the sun is
    high,
But when it is dark he wants a roof to keep away the sky.

If you call a gypsy a vagabond I think you do him wrong,
For he never goes a-travelling but he takes his home along.
And the only reason a road is good, as every wanderer knows,
Is just because of the homes, the homes, the homes to which it
    goes.

They say that life is a highway and its milestones are the years,
And now and then there's a toll-gate where you buy your way
    with tears.
It's a rough road and a steep road and it stretches broad and
    far,
But at last it leads to a golden Town where golden Houses are.

—Joyce Kilmer

2. DELIGHT IN FOOD

My parents spent their honeymoon at Lake View House, Gale, N.Y. Looking at my father's letter to his mother, dated June 11, 1908, I am amused to see his ebullient remark about the way he and my mother-to-be were being fed: "The food is excellent—think of brook trout and wheat cakes for breakfast!" The amusement arises from my memory of what my mother told me about the stay at the Lake View House, which extended well on into the summer, at least through most of July. I remember my mother looking meditatively at a roundish, somewhat pink mark on my arm, and saying: "No, Kenton, I don't think that's a strawberry, it's probably a raspberry and comes from the time I was carrying you, in Gale, New York, at that boarding house. When we were first there, the food was varied and plentiful, and your Dad enjoyed it very much. But we stayed a long time, and more people came, and the supply of food seemed to diminish. Your Dad and I got hungrier and hungrier, and we used to go out in the fields and pick raspberries and eat them, until we got thoroughly sick and tired of raspberries. That's probably why you don't like raspberries now. And they must have marked you!"

Dad's next-to-last letter to his mother from Gale, when she was on a visit to England, treats amusingly of the matter of raspberries (the letter is undated except for the year, 1908): "Aline is making raspberry jam. Pray for it, for it is in tribulation. It is being made on a wood fire, which occasionally blazes up, and occasionally goes out. We picked the berries this morning. She is going to put up some blackberries and some huckleberries, and has expressed insane desires to make mixtures after your manner. I curb her with difficulty and an axe."

Writing from New Brunswick, where he and my mother were spending "a week or so" visiting his father, in a letter dated August 4, 1908, my father revels in a vacation from raspberries: "Aline is experimenting in cookery. She has made biscuits, cookies and corn pudding, and is going to put up some peaches."

What might be termed a "gustatory gusto" was characteristic of my Dad. It shows up in letter after letter, in

18

his expressions of appreciation for edible gifts, and in his accounts of cookery and of meals. In 1909 he wrote his mother from Morristown: "The candy was darn good—I never ate any grape fruit peel candied before, and like it much better than candied orange peel." Some of my memories of Dad are of his activities in kitchen and dining room. He used to take pride in his preparation of salads, for instance, and I remember his carefully measuring teaspoonfuls, or part-teaspoonfuls, of powdered mustard, of salt and pepper, and I don't know what other herbs and spices, with appropriate amounts of vinegar, olive or perhaps other oils, and sometimes lemon juice and grated lemon peel. He would arrange his salad in the bowl, with due attention to its attractive appearance, and serve it proudly with his home-made dressing. I remember, too, his distress when he experimented with the boiling of an eggplant, and then tried to skin it. The skin came off in distinct and isolated patches, giving it a leprous appearance at which he shuddered. Mother helped him to tame the eggplant, and bring it to a more healthy look. His dream of living in the lap of luxury was "steak for breakfast."

When I think of my father as I, a young child, knew him, one of the most persistent feelings is the enthusiasm, which I shared with him, for food and drink. He had a romantic and celebrational appreciation for their enjoyment, and for the enjoyment of sharing them with friends and family. This feeling is often apparent in his letters, and occasionally in his poems and other writings. Though I admired the drama of his way of arranging and serving the salad, I seldom participated, since at my age, I neither wanted nor was given salad, as a general rule. But drink was a different matter. I thoroughly enjoyed my official position (in the bosom of the family) as finisher of Dad's bottle of beer. I remember the kinds of beer he usually drank—Jacob Ruppert's Knickerbocker Beer, and, as a luxurious import, Bass's Pale Ale. There was, naturally, only a drop or so in the bottom of the bottle, after he had poured the beer or ale into his glass, but I was delighted to be permitted to drain that last drop or so.

I remember, too, in Larchmont, that Dad somehow had the opportunity to buy a little keg of claret (I suppose nowadays it would be called Bordeaux). I took note of how Dad took care to read directions and follow them precisely. He

19

placed the keg in the prescribed position in the house, and took no drop of wine until the prescribed time had elapsed. I have thought of this in watching John Gielgud's commercial for Paul Masson wines. I was fascinated to see how the spigot served at once as a cork and as a faucet—keeping the wine in, when it was not being served, but letting out a thin, dark red stream of wine when the faucet was opened. As I recall, I was happy to be given a taste, now and then, but didn't much like it.

In his poem, "Delicatessen," Dad expressed his feeling about drinking together as an expression of friendship:

> And there are those who grasp his hand,
> Who drink with him and wish him well.
> O in no drear and lonely land
> Shall he who honors friendship dwell.

It is in "Delicatessen," also that Dad expressed most eloquently his delight in different kinds of food, and in thinking of where each kind came from, and how it was prepared.

He also had a feeling for individual tastes and preferences. I remember the mention of such a preference in his short story, "Whitemail" which was published in *Smart Set* in 1914, and reprinted in *Ellery Queen's Mystery Magazine* in January, 1952. My memory is all the more vivid because I definitely do not share the taste, and I doubt if Dad did. It was just the taste of his fictional narrator. "Soon," the story goes, "we were comfortably seated at a table in Jimmy's bar. Jimmy, I was absurdly pleased to notice, remembered me and put a few drops of syrup in my Irish, as if I were still a daily visitor."

I don't know how it happens that that story, "Whitemail," is not included in Dad's published books. I do think it may be in *The Smart Set Anthology*. (For correct book title and date, as well as for inclusion of that story, I'd have to check in a library). It's a good story, with a surprise ending, and I guess we can stand a little gulp of Irish whisky with syrup in it. (I wonder if that was maple syrup?)

In Dad's letters to his mother, food keeps cropping up. Also, often, some sort of ceremonial enters into his expressed enjoyment of the food. In 1909, for instance (his letters are hardly ever given more specific dates), he wrote to her: "I have got a job with Funk & Wagnalls, the publishers of *The Literary Digest*... If I don't like that job—or if Funk & Wagnalls don't like me—I have a chance to enter the book department of Scribner's on Sept. 1st. In either case we will live in New York which ought to gratify you. We will take you to dinner at the Café Boulevard, where they have an amiable roof garden and a Hungarian orchestra in costume, and a man with a mandolin, who sings in Hungarian and Italian."

In another 1909 letter, announcing to his mother where his new office is, and looking forward to her returning from England and lunching with him in New York, he says: "We will go to Dorlon's, which is next door to my office, or to Cavanagh's, which is only two blocks off, or to the restaurant in the basement of the Flatiron Building, which is on the next corner. I have discovered an amiable drink, which I am eager to see you consume. It consists of equal parts of French Vermouth and Cassis, and is served in a cocktail glass."

Some time in 1910, probably early March, Dad wrote to his mother about celebrating my birthday, not on the precise day, which was March 21, but on Easter Sunday, March 27. In this letter he refers to me, over and over, as "Puff." The name reminds me of a conversation I had with my mother, in Mahwah, probably about 1913 or 1914. I couldn't remember what nickname he had been calling me by, and asked if he called me "Buster," which was a name I had heard someone use, but Mother told me Dad never called me Buster, but did call me Puff. Naturally, I asked why he called me that. She said it was a name he had called me before I was born, as a term suitable to girl or boy, and expressive of her shape in those days! So, after I was born, I remained Puff to him, on occasion.

To return, for the moment, to the subject of Dad's enjoyment of food, I like to think of his advice to his mother in England, in a letter for once fully dated, "April 20, 1914": "Eat English mustard on roast beef, and lemon juice on chops. Drink a mixture of white créme de menthe and brandy before meals, since English cocktails are bad."

21

3. TRACING RELATIONSHIPS AND
FRIENDSHIPS THROUGH TIME

Sometimes my memories of my father are, as I think I have mentioned before, memories of things I have been told, rather than direct recollections. Some of these actually go back to times, not only before my birth, but even before my father's birth. I take particular pleasure in such family memories that link my father's family with my mother's, and that link friends of about a century back with my own personal experience. One link, that does stem from my own memory, is that my grandmother, Annie Kilburn Kilmer, once remarked to me that her mother's mother, Hulda Curtis Smith, was cousin to George William Curtis, so I'll insert his identification from William Rose Benét's *Reader's Encyclopedia*. "(1824-1892) American author and journalist. Member of Brook Farm Community (1842-1843); editorial writer for *Harper's Magazine* and editor of *Harper's Weekly*. Author of *Potiphar Papers* (1853), *Prue and I* (1857), etc."

The connection here is that, while George William Curtis was writing editorials for *Harper's Magazine*, my Grandaddy, my mother's step-father, Henry Mills Alden, was editor of that magazine. Curtis's editorials were familiar essays, under the general heading, "The Editor's Easy Chair," and Henry Mills Alden wrote more solemn pieces, called "The Editor's Study." I have in my library a book by Curtis, *From the Easy Chair*, inscribed "H. M. Alden, from his faithful loge, The Easy Chair. Christmas, 1891."

How memories crop up in later life! When I was working in the Library of Congress, somewhere in the nineteen-fifties, in what was then called the Legislative Reference Service (now Congressional Research), a new man joined the staff, Dr. Arthur Devan. He told me he had been my father's friend and classmate at Rutgers. I couldn't remember our first meeting, when I was less than a year old, but I well remembered a passage from a 1909 letter from Dad to his mother, in which, after saying "God help the druggist who decks his window after my suggestions," he went on: "Speaking of God, Arthur Devan called last night. He was much embarrassed when Kenton appeared in his nightgown to greet him. When he departed, Arthur shook hands with Aline and remarked,

'Good night, Buster!' immediately turning purple and explaining that he meant Kenton, and not Aline, by this laudatory title."

As it has been said that our most vividly remembered episodes are those that involve our embarrassments, I never mentioned this memory to Dr. Devan, who became my good friend and valued colleague.

Another Library of Congress memory, reaching even farther back in time, is of the occasion when an old gentleman, as white-haired as I am now, approached me in my then position in the Microfilm Reading Room. Having made sure that I was indeed Kenton Kilmer, he told me that in his college days, at Rutgers, he used to frequent Dr. Kilmer's Opera House Drugstore for his sodas and malted milks.

Another, more complicated, connection comes up with the name of Sarah Corbin, who taught my father in Rutgers Preparatory School when he was about twelve.She may have been my mother's teacher also. In any case, she became a family friend of incredibly long standing. I remember, when I myself was in high school (Georgetown Preparatory School), and visiting my New Brunswick grandparents on a vacation, that my grandmother took me to visit Sarah Coerr (Mrs. Rutherford L. Coerr), in the nearby town of Metuchen, who had been Sarah Corbin before her second marriage. Among Dad's letters to his mother there are occasional mentions of visits to the Corbins. In a letter dated "1909" (an irritating custom for one trying to establish a sequence of events), Dad wrote, after telling of rescuing a cigar from me, when I was beginning to eat it "I stopped him, as it was a good cigar," he wrote: "Aline and I dined with the Corbins last Wednesday. Sflager said she had a letter from you and intended to write soon. She is looking very well now. She sleeps out on a balcony."

In writing about the Corbins, Dad regularly refers to one of them as "Sflager." I suppose this refers to some happening back in his school days, when either he or a schoolmate misread or miswrote the name "Sarah" as "Sflager." I wish I had thought to ask her about it during our correspondence in the 1940's. The letter from which I've been quoting seems to have been written when Mother and Dad had left Morristown, but not yet moved to their New York boarding house, and the

23

address at the head of the letter is the family home at 147 College Avenue in New Brunswick.

My mother and I saw Sarah Coerr at Granny's funeral, and undertook to try to keep in touch thereafter. Among my mother's papers that I have given to the Georgetown University Library is a pair of postcards, postmarked Aug. 26 and Sep. 10, 1941. The first of these, sent from New York, says: —Bessie Burr writes me that she has seen you—and that's next best to seeing you myself. If the restrictions on gasoline are not too severe, perhaps I may be able to grasp your hand on our return from Ocean Beach. Love to you always. Sarah C." The second has the note: "Just a message of affection from Fire Id. Sarah Coerr. We go home this week."

While I was living with my mother in Stillwater, in the early 1930's, we used to exchange Christmas cards and other occasional notes with Sarah Coerr, and, naturally, when I became engaged to Frances Frieseke, either Mother or I wrote to tell her that news. On June 2, 1937, Frances and I were married in Le Mesnil sur Blangy, Calvados, France, and Sarah Coerr responded with enthusiasm and affection to that news. Thereafter, we kept in touch still by Christmas cards, and, in the course of time, with our birth announcements. I don't remember in what year Mrs. Coerr died, but I do remember that she kept careful track of our numerous offspring, sending a valentine each year, to each child! The Valentine envelope that arrived from her was pretty well stuffed by the time of the last such message.

It is part of Murphy's laws, I suppose, that the letters you throw away are the ones you are bound to need. I now have only one of the many letters we have received from Sarah Coerr. This is undated, and is sent from her house, Woodstock, Metuchen, New Jersey. It must have been written in 1946, since it is acknowledging receipt of my anthology, *This Is My America*, a collection of poems from *The Washington Post*, which was published in that year. I was poetry editor of the paper from 1940 through 1947, and built the anthology on the framework of a long poem by Lieutenant-Colonel William A. Brewer, that had been featured in the paper, upon my recommendation. Mrs. Coerr had long since adopted the name of "Aunt Sarah" for her letters to Frances and me and our children.

"My dear Kenton: More than you can know, you have pleased me with the gift of your Anthology. Col. Brewer's "This is my America" is inspiring, the poems are genuinely pleasing—each in its own way.—I regret that none of yours is there.—but I am glad to learn of your interests from the note on the jacket.

"That you and yours should adopt me into the family is delightful. I still cherish the artistic (!) specimens of the children's work, and the gracious note of March twenty-eighth from Frances.—

"Looking over the authors' names in your book, I recognize the Goodales.—About sixty years ago, I attended a school entertainment in Reading, Conn., to hear Dora recite "Bingen on the Rhine."—She is niece of my mother's cousin—Elaine had just gone to Minnesota where she was destined to meet her Sioux Indian.—

"Their poems do not satisfy me as do some of the others however.

"Thanking you for your thought of me—and with an affectionate greeting to Frances, and a thought of each of the five (Ada has told me how precious they are).

"Sincerely, Aunt Sarah"

Here again is a connection between my father's history and my mother's. Dora Read Goodale and Elaine Goodale were two sisters, very young, acting as partners in writing poetry. Their first magazine publication, as my mother told me, was in *Harper's Magazine*, and Henry Mills Alden was the first editor to accept their work. Elaine's "Sioux Indian" was Charles Alexander Eastman, and Elaine's later poems were signed "Elaine Goodale Eastman." Dr. Eastman's Indian name was Ohiyesa. I have, from my childhood, the book *Indian Legends Retold*, by Elaine Goodale Eastman, with an introduction by Charles Alexander Eastman.

Some time after their marriage, Dr. and Mrs. Eastman moved to Metuchen, where they were well acquainted with the Alden family, including my mother, Aline Murray.

The Ada here mentioned by Sarah Coerr is my mother's elder sister, Ada Murray Clarke.

Moving forward again for a few decades, I remember when I was at work on a bit of local history for Fairfax County, doing the research that led to the publication of my

25

book, *The Fairfax Family in Fairfax County*, Fairfax, Va., 1965. I was on my way to see my supervisor, Nan Netherton. Seeing a used book store, naturally I stopped, and in it I found, for a ridiculously low price, *Apple Blossoms Poems of Two Children*, Elaine Goodale, Dora Read Goodale, New York, Putnam (c1878). When I went into Mrs. Netherton's office, book in hand, of course she asked, "What have you there?" When I showed her the book, she exclaimed, "Why, *I* knew Dora Read Goodale well! I used to visit her in her home in Tennessee."

Another book that I find in my library is *Mountain Dooryards*, by Dora Read Goodale, Torch Press, Cedar Rapids, Iowa (n.d.). This book contains her poem, "East Wind," that is also included in *This Is My America*, and has my favorable comment on the jacket. I wonder if she and Elaine ever connected me with their early editor, Henry Mills Alden, and with the young girl Elaine knew in Metuchen, Aline Murray?

I hope readers may enjoy, as I do, tracing these threads of relationships through a century and more.

MY MIRROR

There is a mirror in my room
Less like a mirror than a tomb,
There are so many ghosts that pass
Across the surface of the glass.

When in the morning I arise
With circles round my tired eyes,
Seeking the glass to brush my hair
My mother's mother meets me there.

If in the middle of the day
I happen to go by that way,
I see a smile I used to know—
My mother, twenty years ago.

But when I rise by candlelight
To feed my baby in the night,
Then whitely in the glass I see
My dead child's face look out at me.

—Aline Kilmer

TRIBUTE

Deborah and Christopher brought me dandelions,
    Kenton brought me buttercups with summer on their breath,
But Michael brought an autumn leaf, a lacy filigree,
    A wan leaf, a ghost leaf, beautiful as death.

Death in all loveliness, fragile and exquisite,
    Who but he would choose it from all the blossoming land?
Who but he would find it where it hid among the flowers?
    Death in all loveliness, he laid it in my hand.

—Aline Kilmer

AGAINST THE WALL

If I live till my fighting days are done,
I must fasten my armour on my eldest son.

I would give him better, but this is my best.
I can get along without it—I'll be glad to have rest.

And I'll sit mending armour with my back against the wall,
Because I have a second son, if this one should fall.

So I'll make it very shiny and I'll whistle very loud,
And I'll clap him on the shoulder and I'll say, very proud:

    "This is the lance *I* used to bear!"
    But I mustn't tell what happened when I bore it.
    "This is the helmet *I* used to wear!"
    But I won't say what befell me when I wore it.

For you couldn't tell a youngster, it wouldn't be right,
That you wish you had died in your very first fight.

And I mustn't say that victory is never worth the cost,
That defeat may be bitter, but it's better to have lost.

And I mustn't say that glory is barren as a stone.
I'd better not say anything, but leave the lad alone.

So he'll fight very bravely and probably he'll fall:
And I'll sit mending armour with my back against the wall.

                       —Aline Kilmer

FOR THE BIRTHDAY OF A MIDDLE-AGED CHILD

I'm sorry you are wiser,
    I'm sorry you are taller;
I liked you better foolish,
    And I liked you better smaller.
I'm sorry you have learning
    And I hope you won't display it;
But since this is your birthday
    I suppose I mustn't say it.

I liked you with your hair cut
    Like a mediaeval page's,
And I hate to see your eyes change
    From a seraph's to a sage's.
You are not half so beautiful
    Since middle-age befell you;
But since this is your birthday
    I suppose I mustn't tell you.

—Aline Kilmer

EXPERIENCE

Deborah danced, when she was two,
As buttercups and daffodils do;
Spirited, frail, naively bold
Her hair a ruffled crest of gold,
And whenever she spoke her voice went singing
Like water up from a fountain springing.

But now her step is quiet and slow;
She walks the way primroses go;
Her hair is yellow instead of gilt,
Her voice is losing its lovely lilt,
And in place of her wild, delightful ways
A quaint precision rules her days.

For Deborah now is three, and oh,
She knows so much that she did not know.

—Aline Kilmer

CANDLES THAT BURN

Candles that burn for a November birthday,
　　Wreathed round with asters and with goldenrod,
As you go upward in your radiant dying
　　Carry my prayer to God.

Tell Him she is so small and so rebellious,
　　Tell him her words are music on her lips,
Tell Him I love her in her wayward beauty
　　Down to her fingertips.

Ask Him to keep her brave and true and lovely,
　　Vivid and happy, gay as she is now,
Ask Him to let no shadow touch her beauty,
　　No sorrow mar her brow.

All the sweet saints that came for her baptising,
　　Tell them I pray them to be always near.
Ask them to keep her little feet from stumbling,
　　Her gallant heart from fear.

Candles that burn for a November birthday,
　　Wreathed round with asters and with goldenrod,
As you go upward in your radiant dying,
　　Carry my prayer to God.

—Aline Kilmer

"A WIND IN THE NIGHT"

A wind rose in the night,
    (She had always feared it so!)
Sorrow plucked at my heart
    And I could not help but go.

Softly I went and stood
    By her door at the end of the hall.
Dazed with grief I watched
    The candles flaring and tall.

The wind was wailing aloud:
    I thought how she would have cried
For my warm familiar arms
    And the sense of me by her side.

The candles flickered and leapt,
    The shadows jumped on the wall.
She lay before me small and still
    And did not care at all.

—Aline Kilmer

ATONEMENT

When a storm comes up at night and the wind is crying,
    When the trees are moaning like masts on labouring ships,
I wake in fear and put out my hand to find you,
    With your name on my lips.

No pain that the heart can hold is like to this one—
    To call, forgetting, into aching space,
To reach out confident hands and find beside you
    Only an empty place.

This should atone for the hours when I forget you.
    Take then my offering, clean and sharp and sweet,
An agony brighter than years of dull remembrance.
    I lay it at your feet.

                        —Aline Kilmer

AFTER GRIEVING

When I was young I was so sad!
   I was so sad! I did not know
Why any living thing was glad
   When one must some day sorrow so.
      But now that grief has come to me
      My heart is like a bird set free.

I always knew that it would come;
   I always felt it waiting there;
Its shadow kept my glad voice dumb
   And crushed my gay soul with despair.
      But now that I have lived with grief
      I feel an exquisite relief.

Runners who know their proven strength,
   Ships that have shamed the hurricane:
These are my brothers, and at length
   I shall come back to joy again.
      However hard my life may be
      I know it shall not conquer me.

—Aline Kilmer

I SHALL NOT BE AFRAID

I shall not be afraid any more,
    Either by night or day;
What would it profit me to be afraid
    With you away?

Now I am brave. In the dark night alone
    All through the house I go,
Locking the doors and making windows fast
    When sharp winds blow.

For there is only sorrow in my heart;
    There is no room for fear.
But how I wish I were afraid again,
    My dear, my dear!

—Aline Kilmer

4. READING AND WRITING AND POEM RECITING

Like most children of my time, the early years of the twentieth century, I saw a lot more of my mother, Aline Kilmer, than of my father. Some of my most vivid memories of my mother are of her reading to me, or saying poems. The one poem that I remember my father saying to me was this one:

> Feast on wine, or fast on water
>   And your honour shall stand sure:
> God Almighty's son and daughter—
>   He the stalwart, she the pure;
> If an angel out of Heaven
>   Bring you other things to drink—
> Thank him for his kind intentions;
>   Go and pour them down the sink!

Though I was sure this was by either G.K. Chesterton or Hilaire Belloc, I had a time finding it. Our daughter Miriam remembered it from convent reading at meals! It was quoted in Theodore Maynard's autobiography, *The World I Saw*, and that book was read, chapter by chapter, to nuns and novices, in the convent she was preparing to join. Maynard credits it to G.K. Chesterton, and identifies it as in his high-hearted book, *The Flying Inn*.

In contrast, I remember my mother's saying so many poems to me that I despair of ever listing them all. She gave me narrative poems suitable to my age, through my early childhood, and a good many of them, finding how much I enjoyed them, she would say over from time to time. Of these, I remember particularly Longfellow's "Paul Revere's Ride," and "The Wreck of the Hesperus," Jean Ingelow's "High Tide on the Coast of Lincolnshire," Robert Browning's "The Pied Piper of Hamelin," Mary Howitt's "The Spider and the Fly," (sometimes she *sang* that one to me and the younger children), Robert Southey's "The Inchcape Rock," and many of Walter De la Mare's poems from *Peacock Pie*. As I grew older, she would say Shakespeare's and Milton's sonnets, Shelley's and Keats's Odes, and many poems by the poets of the nineteen-twenties. When I think of Strickland Gillilan's poem, "I Had a Mother Who Read to Me," I think of my own mother, and how

37

she not only read to me, but gave me immeasurable riches out of the storehouse of her poetic memory.

In her reading to me, Mother used a device that my wife and I, in turn, have found very useful in getting children to *want* to read in the first place, and to learn to read with hardly any difficulty. It's very simple. Hold the child on your lap as you read, and the child looks at the pictures (of course for a young child it must be well and copiously illustrated). Very soon, the child begins to recognize the words and learn how to sound the letters. I learned to read when I was three, had to go without reading for a while on account of an eye infection, and then took it up again easily.

I remember one episode very early in my reading career. Mother was doing some household task that would allow her to read to me at the same time, and she sent me upstairs to get a book of stories she knew I would like. She told me to look for, and bring down, a book called *Our Island Saints*. After a long search, I came down shamefaced, and told her I couldn't find it, but that I *had* found a book called *Our Izland Saints*. I wondered if that could be the book she meant. So she had to explain to me about the occasional spelling trap called the "silent letter." Then she went ahead and read to me about St. David, or St. Patrick, or whatever other saint she chose to read about that day.

I remember how Mother used to sit in an armchair, with one child in her lap, and others gathered round where we could see the words and pictures, and read books like Mother Goose rhymes, Stevenson's *Child's Garden of Verses*, or other poems suitable to our range of ages. Obviously, not *every* child can be in a lap, when there are several to be read to, but Mother worked out a good compromise.

My sister, who was Deborah long ago and is now Sister Michael, recently reminded me to tell of a happening Mother used to mention to us now and then, to show how tired she had sometimes been with the combination of child care, housework, and sometimes helping Dad by typing his interviews, lectures, and other writings. One late afternoon Dad came home from his work in New York, and told Mother (or reminded her) that they were to go out to dinner. So while he straightened his tie, or some such minor adjustment, she went up to the bedroom to change into the kind of dress ladies wore to dinner in those times. As she got out of her housedress, however, sleepiness and habit overcame her, and she got all undressed and put on her nightgown. When Dad began to get impatient about her non-appearance, and went up to the bedroom, he found her fast asleep in bed!

To return for a moment to the subject of spelling, and related matters, I cherish the story Mother used to tell about her mortifying experience in school in New Jersey, when, at the age of twelve, she had just been brought up from Norfolk, on account of her mother's marriage to Henry Mills Alden, who lived in Metuchen. The teacher, checking the familiarity of the pupils with the use of the indefinite article, asked for an example of a use of "a" rather than "an." Mother confidently gave as an example, "a possum." Universal laughter from the class, all New Jersey children being aware that the animal was "an opossum"!

Dad and Mother were a couple very much in love, as is evident from their poems. Their marriage was very definitely a partnership, in writing as well as in the care of the family. If there were ever any disagreements between them about the treatment of us children, those disagreements were settled out of our sight and hearing. In writing, Mother was not only Dad's occasional typist, since she used the professional ten-finger style, and Dad the "newspaper man" two-finger hunt and peck method, but she was regularly consulted about matters of style and content, in Dad's prose writings as well as in his poetry. Dad similarly discussed Mother's writings with her, helping when help was needed.

One of my happy memories is the dramatic effect with which Granny, Annie Kilburn Kilmer, used to recite Dad's poems, such as "The House with Nobody In It" and "Roofs." She put tears in her voice as she said: "For I can't help thinking the poor old house is a house with a broken heart." In reciting "Roofs," she gave full value to the crescendo needed in the lines:

> And the only reason a road is good, as every wanderer knows,
> Is just because of the homes, the homes, the homes to
> which it goes.

It is no wonder that, after Dad's death, she was much in demand as a performer, more than reciter, of his poetry.

IN MEMORY

I

Serene and beautiful and very wise,
   Most erudite in curious Grecian lore,
   You lay and read your learned books, and bore
A weight of unshed tears and silent sighs.
The song within your heart could never rise
   Until love bade it spread its wings and soar.
   Nor could you look on Beauty's face before
A poet's burning mouth had touched your eyes.

Love is made out of ecstasy and wonder;
   Love is a poignant and accustomed pain.
It is a burst of Heaven-shaking thunder;
   It is a linnet's fluting after rain.
Love's voice is through your song, above and under
   And in each note to echo and remain.

II

Because Mankind is glad and brave and young,
   Full of gay flames that white and scarlet glow,
   All joys and passions that mankind may know
By you were nobly felt and nobly sung.
Because Mankind's heart every day is wrung
   By Fate's wild hands that twist and tear it so,
   Therefore you echoed Man's undying woe,
A harp Aeolian on Life's branches hung.

So did the ghosts of toiling children hover
   About the piteous portals of your mind;
Your eyes, that looked on glory, could discover
   The angry scar to which the world was blind:
And it was grief that made Mankind your lover,
   And it was grief that made you love Mankind.

III

Before Christ left the Citadel of Light,
   To tread the dreadful way of human birth,
   His shadow sometimes fell upon the earth
And those who saw it wept with joy and fright.

"Thou are Apollo, than the sun more bright!"
  They cried. "Our music is of little worth,
  But thrill our blood with thy creative mirth,
Thou god of song, thou lord of lyric might!"

O singing pilgrim! who could love and follow
  Your lover Christ, through even love's despair,
You knew within the cypress-darkened hollow
  The feet that on the mountain are so fair.
For it was Christ that was your own Apollo,
  And thorns were in the laurel on your hair.

—Joyce Kilmer

41

AS WINDS THAT BLOW AGAINST A STAR

(For Aline)

Now by what whim of wanton chance
　　Do radiant eyes know sombre days?
And feet that shod in light should dance
　　Walk weary and laborious ways?

But rays from Heaven, white and whole,
　　May penetrate the gloom of earth;
And tears but nourish, in your soul,
　　The glory of celestial mirth.

The darts of toil and sorrow, sent
　　Against your peaceful beauty, are
As foolish and as impotent
　　As winds that blow against a star.

—Joyce Kilmer

SONG

Love goes
As the wind blows,
And no man knows
    The place thereof.
But pity stays
Through weary days
    Keeping the house of Love.

Though you come late
To the swinging gate,
The path is straight
    And the door is wide,
And Pity's eyes
Are so sadly wise
    You will think it is Love inside.

—Aline Kilmer

THE PROUD POET (Excerpt)

(For Shaemas O'Sheel)

It is stern work, it is perilous work, to thrust your hand in the
    sun
  And pull out a spark of immortal fire to warm the hearts of
    men:
But Prometheus, torn by the claws and beaks whose task is
    never done,
  Would be tortured another eternity to go stealing fire again.

—Joyce Kilmer

FATHER GERARD HOPKINS, S.J.

Why didst thou carve they speech laboriously,
    And match and blend thy words with curious art?
    For Song, one saith, is but a human heart
Speaking aloud, undisciplined and free.
Nay, God be praised, Who fixed thy task for thee!
    austere, ecstatic craftsman, set apart
    From all who traffic in Apollo's mart,
On thy phrased paten shall the Splendour be!

Now, carelessly, we throw a rhyme to God,
    Singing His praise when other songs are done.
But thou, who knewest paths Teresa trod,
    Losing thyself, what is it thou hast won?
O bleeding feet, with peace and glory shod!
    O happy moth, that flew into the Sun!

—Joyce Kilmer

IN MEMORY OF RUPERT BROOKE

In alien earth, across a troubled sea,
    His body lies that was so fair and young.
    His mouth is stopped, with half his songs unsung;
His arm is still, that struck to make men free.
But let no cloud of lamentation be
    Where, on a warrior's grave, a lyre is hung.
    We keep the echoes of his golden tongue,
We keep the vision of his chivalry.

So Israel's joy, the loveliest of kings,
    Smote now his harp, and now the hostile horde.
To-day the starry roof of Heaven rings
    With psalms a soldier made to praise his Lord;
And David rests beneath Eternal wings,
    Song on his lips, and in his hand a sword.

—Joyce Kilmer

MOONLIGHT

The moon reached in cold hands across the sill
 And touched me as I lay sleeping;
And in my sleep I thought of sorrowful things:
 I wakened, and I lay weeping.

I could hear on the beach below the small waves break
 And fall on the silver shingle,
And the sound of a footstep passing in the street
 Where lamplight and moonlight mingle.

And I said: "All day I can turn my face to the sun
 And lead my thoughts to laughter;
But I hope in my heart that I never shall sleep again
 Because of the pain thereafter."

The moon's pale fingers wandered across my face
 And the arm where my hot cheek rested,
And because of the tears in my eyes I could not see
 Where the black waves rocked moon-crested.

         —Aline Kilmer

5. POETRY: FUN AND FURY

Many memories I have of my father are, since I was only eight when he sailed for France, and nine when he died, actually memories of what my mother told me. Consequently, I seem to remember his Columbia University years, long before I was born, as well as much that happened in my childhood, and in my presence. I remember directly how he could be at once intimidatingly fierce and affectionately funny. Sometimes I felt I just didn't know how to handle a Dad like that! My mother told me a story that I remember well, about how he hated to get up in the morning. (That World War I song using the phrase must have appealed to him.) When he was in the Delta Upsilon Fraternity House at Columbia University, my mother said, his fraternity brothers used to cast lots for the privilege of waking him, on account of "the interesting things he would say."

A remembered story from the Columbia days is about Carlos Wupperman, a fellow student, and Professor Jackson (what he was teaching I don't know). Wupperman for some reason was very angry with Professor Jackson, and was refusing to speak to him or in any way acknowledge his existence. One day, encountering Professor Jackson on a walk through the campus of Columbia University, Carlos Wupperman tipped his hat. Dad, observing this earthshaking event, was moved to celebrate it in deathless verse:

When Wupperman takes off his hat to Professor Jackson,
     All the people say:
"When Wupperman takes off his hat to Professor Jackson,
     It's a lovely day!"

Another thing I remember about Dad's ferocity is from a comment my mother made to me about a much-admired poem of his,

Thanksgiving
The roar of the world is in my ears.
     Thank God for the roar of the world!
Thank God for the mighty tide of fears
     Against me always hurled!

Thank God for the bitter and ceaseless strife,
     And the sting of His chastening rod!

48

Thank God for the stress and the pain of life,
And Oh, thank God for God!

My mother said that she was never able to appreciate that
poem to the full, because she remembered so vividly that, at
the time he was writing the poem, the roar that was in her ears
was *his* roar. Their bedroom, in the Mahwah house, was at the
same time his office.

TO A YOUNG POET WHO KILLED HIMSELF

When you had played with life a space
    And made it drink and lust and sing,
You flung it back into God's face
    And thought you did a noble thing.
"Lo, I have lived and loved," you said,
    "And sung to fools too dull to hear me.
Now for a cool and grassy bed
    With violets in blossom near me."

Well, rest is good for weary feet,
    Although they ran for no great prize;
And violets are very sweet,
    Although their roots are in your eyes.
But hark to what the earthworms say
    Who share with you your muddy haven:
"The fight was on—you ran away.
    You are a coward and a craven.

"The rug is ruined where you bled;
    It was a dirty way to die!
To put a bullet through your head
    And make a silly woman cry!
You could not vex the merry stars
    Nor make them heed you, dead or living.
Not all your puny anger mars
    God's irresistible forgiving.

"Yes, God forgives and men forget,
    And you're forgiven and forgotten.
You might be gaily sinning yet
    And quick and fresh instead of rotten.
And when you think of love and fame
    And all that might have come to pass,
Then don't you feel a little shame?
    And don't you think you were an ass?"

—Joyce Kilmer

6. FUN WITH BOOKS

In writing about my parents, I must emphasize the fact that the love of books was surely one of the factors, both in their meeting and getting along together in Rutgers Prep, and in their later relationship that brought about and enriched their family life. In Annie Kilburn Kilmer's *Memories of My Son*, there is an illustration of my Dad in the character of Sydney Carton, in *A Tale of Two Cities*. Somewhere in my house, I have a photograph of Granny in the character of Sairey Gamp, in *Martin Chuzzlewit*. The acting out of plays, of stories, and of chapters of stories, was a favorite recreation in the New Brunswick household of Granny and Grandad. Whether Grandad joined in, I don't know, but I remember hearing of dramatic readings in which my mother, young Aline Murray, participated, and also of some in which her younger sister, Constance (later Constance Murray Greene) took part. I have heard both Granny and Constance laugh over the delicate, ladylike tone in which Mother had pronounced the sepulchral line of the Ghost. "Avenge this foul and most unnatural murder!" Mother herself remembered it in a shamefaced, but still amused, fashion. After Dad and Mother were married, I believe these dramatic readings continued, on the occasions when Mother and Dad visited Dad's parents.

Dickens was a regular favorite for these readings, as shown by the photographs I have mentioned, and Granny's and Dad's fondness for Dickens was indicated by the fact that each of them served, Granny long after Dad's death, as President of the Dickens Fellowship in New York. A complete set of Dickens, The Gadshill Edition, in thirty-four volumes, with the two-volume Forster *Life of Charles Dickens*, is on the shelves in our dining room. I look in vain for a publication date in those volumes, but I am sure they were a proud possession of my mother and father when they had few other books; and that they were much read I have personal knowledge. Through the years from my early childhood to my twenties, Mother and I, and sometimes my siblings, used to read aloud to one another, or to the family group. Very often the choice was a Dickens book—either an often-read and much loved one, or one we'd never read or heard. Many other standard authors, among the English novelists, served for

51

these readings aloud—Scott, Thackeray, George Eliot, Kipling, George Meredith, Thomas Hardy. I remember, too, how in later years, Mother and I would read to each other when either one was involved in a task not requiring full concentration. We would take up the writings of one particular author, borrowing his or her books from a library, and read through all we could find of that author. Many of these were translations from various languages, like the Polish stories of Sienkiewicz and the many historical romances of Alexandre Dumas.

Of the set of George Eliot, I remember my mother's remark, when she visited us once in our house in Arlington, that she and Dad had the custom, whenever they moved, of putting that George Eliot set in a carefully chosen spot on a bookshelf. Once that was done, they felt that they were at home, and would proceed to arrange other books, and their furniture. Sets of Thackeray and Scott are similarly valued, as their stories have, through the years, been enjoyed by our family members, whether in solitary reading or in reading aloud.

In my house, I see constant reminders of both my father and my mother, not only in the photographs of both, hanging in our bedroom, but also in books just about everywhere in the house. A book I happened to come across on our bookshelves yesterday reminded me of one matter on which they never got together completely—the matter of foreign languages. The book in question is a school textbook, *Episodes from Tales of the Black Forest*, Berthold Auerbach, edited with notes by A. H. Fox Strangways, M.A., London, Longmans, Green, 1890. On the fly-leaf, in a decorative black printing characteristic of my father, is the inscription, "Aline Kilmer's Book." The text is, of course, in German. We have also Dad's sets of Goethe and Schiller, well-worn and well-read. Despite Dad's best efforts, Mother never did learn German well enough to enjoy reading it, nor do I remember her ever reading French, though I know Dad read and admired many French poets, such as Verlaine and Paul Fort, whose paperback books I have inherited from Dad. Since my wife, Frances Frieseke, is bilingual, and lived in France until I went over there and married her, we have many books in French that may or may not have belonged to Dad. One of his most moving poems is "The Cathedral of Rheims, (From the French of Emile Verhaeren)." I remember that Mother had no difficulty in reading any letter in French that she might receive, and it did happen sometimes, and she occasionally sang both French and German folksongs. Her reading in foreign languages, however, ran more to Latin and Greek than to French (German being out of the question for her). I remember her expressing gratification in having succeeded in translating a brief Greek quatrain: To Aphrodite: With a Mirror.

Here, Cyprian, is my jewelled looking-glass,
  My final gift to bind my final vow:
I cannot see myself as I once was;
  I would not see myself as I am now.

She was proud to feel that in this translation she had surpassed Matthew Prior, whose version of the same quatrain is:

The Lady who offers her Looking-Glass to Venus
  Venus, take my votive glass:
  Since I am not what I was,
  What from this day I shall be,
  Venus, let me never see.

With regard to translations from the Greek, I have another "memory" from my mother's school days. They were studying Homer, and Mother translated a Homeric phrase as "the sail-winged sea." She felt happy with the phrase, but the teacher shouted: "No, no! The sea covered with sails as if with wings." Mother told me of this with amusement, but a lasting bitterness.

On our bookshelves, there are many and varied inscriptions. One of these, particularly cherished, is a forged one! My mother's mother, Ada Alden, picked out and gave to me *Contemporary Scottish Verse*, edited by...Sir George Douglas, Bart., which is a volume in The Canterbury Poets, Edited by William Sharp. William Sharp, well known as an editor and writer, is remembered also as the secret identity behind the nom de plume of the poet and novelist, Fiona Macleod. Gran, in giving me the book, pointed out that it was inscribed: "To Mrs. Alden, with the affectionate regard of William Sharp. Pludgwick: Sussex: 23:9:93." Regretting that the date indicated that the inscription must be addressed to the *first*

Mrs. Alden, Gran took a sharp penknife and carefully removed the tail of the final nine in the date. Now it reads "23:9:03"!

"Well," she said, "he knew me just as well as he knew her, and he *might* have inscribed the book to me."

Another kind of inscription enshrines the manner in which books, and particularly poetry books, linked my father and mother. When Dad had a poem accepted and paid for, he used to buy Mother a book, usually a book of poems, with the money he got for the poem. Then he would write on a fly-leaf her name, the date, and the initials, or initial, of the title of the poem. One example is the two-volume set of the *Collected Poems* of Austin Dobson. The inscription, in the first volume, reads: "Aline Kilmer, February the eighteenth, Nineteen hundred and eleven. T. D. L." The poem meant is presumably "The Dead Lover," one of the early poems included in Dad's first book of poems, *Summer of Love*.

Books so given and inscribed were not always on the highest esthetic plane. One I recently donated to the Kilmer Papers in the Georgetown University Library was *Bab Ballads*, by William Schwenk Gilbert, and the inscription indicated that the poem whose proceeds were used for it was "M." That could be "Matin," "Martin," "Madness," or "Metamorphosis." To identify it for sure, one would have to check the publication date of that poem against the date of the inscription— presumably not quite the same date, but close, as journals usually pay a little while after publication date.

Mother used to enjoy telling of her ridiculous youthful mistakes, like that matter of the *o*possum. One of these had to do with a book. She told me she read almost all the way through a book called *Polish Blood* before she realized that the title didn't have to do with polish, as in shoe polish or silver polish, but with the blood of Polish people, as spilled in battle. She said as she read the book she kept wondering about what "polish" had to do with it! From both my mother and my father I learned, early, that all sorts of fun could be had from books—even the fun of finding one's own absurd mistakes.

Some years ago, a daughter, then very young, remarked with glee: "I've found a poem that says 'Excelsior' *nine* times! That triumphant exclamation reminded me of the time my mother had recited Longfellow's "Excelsior" to me, prompting me to ask a question about the lines:

A youth who bore, 'mid snow and ice,
A banner with the strange device,
Excelsior!

"Mother," I asked, "How could he expect to find excelsior by boring through snow and ice? and what was he going to do with it if he found it?"

For present-day readers, it may be advisable to mention that "excelsior" was a packing material, made of wood shaved so very thin that the strips were curly and flexible. As we had recently moved out of Mahwah, I had done a lot of playing with the excelsior many of our breakables had been packed in. If I hadn't thought I knew what "boring" meant, and what "excelsior" meant, I wouldn't have made that ridiculous mistake. But now I'm glad to enjoy my funny misconception.

THE GIFT

He has taken away the things that I loved best:
    Love and youth and the harp that knew my hand.
Laughter alone is left of all the rest.
        Does He mean that I may fill my days with laughter,
    Or will it, too, slip through my fingers like spilt sand?

Why should I beat my wings like a bird in a net,
    When I can be still and laugh at my own desire?
The wise may shake their heads at me, but yet
        I should be sad without my little laughter.
    The crackling of thorns is not so bad a fire.

Will He take away even the thorns from under the pot,
    And send me cold and supperless to bed?
He has been good to me. I know He will not.
        He gave me to keep a little foolish laughter.
    I shall not lose it even when I am dead.

—Aline Kilmer

LOVE'S LANTERN

(For Aline)

Because the road was steep and long
   And through a dark and lonely land,
God set upon my lips a song,
   And put a lantern in my hand.

Through miles on weary miles of night
   That stretch relentless in my way
My lantern burns serene and white,
   An unexhausted cup of day.

O golden lights and lights like wine,
   How dim your boasted splendours are.
Behold this little lamp of mine;
   It is more starlike than a star!

—Joyce Kilmer

VISION

(For Aline)

Homer, they tell us, was blind and could not see the beautiful faces
    Looking up into his own and reflecting the joy of his dream,
    Yet did he seem
Gifted with eyes that could follow the gods to their holiest places.

I have no vision of gods, not of Eros with love-arrows laden,
    Jupiter thundering death or of Juno his white-breasted queen,
    Yet have I seen
All of the joy of the world in the innocent heart of a maiden.

—Joyce Kilmer

PTOLEMAIC

When Ptolemy sat watching from his roof
    The great stars moving through the purple night
He knew that they went swinging round the earth:
    And I believe that Ptolemy was right.

I know the moon is but a silver disc
    Blown across heaven. You see it blowing plainly.
I know the world has towering walls of brass
    Round which the seas of all the earth beat vainly.

The heaven I know is a me decent cover
    Than your infinitude of yawning space.
What have you gained by making things all over
    Into a most intolerable place?

—Aline Kilmer

FAVETE LINGUIS

Speak not the word that turns the flower to ashes,
    Praise not the beauty passing as you gaze.
Let your eyes drink of loveliness in silence:
    It will but wither even as you praise.

See there the plum tree heavy with its blossom
    Swings like the full moon, glimmering and round:
You lift your lute to celebrate its beauty
    And all its petals flutter to the ground.

—Aline Kilmer

7. DISAPPOINTMENTS—AND A GLAD SURPRISE

Some of my most vivid memories of my father are of his reactions to disappointment, especially of times when he tried to do something to give particular joy to me, and somehow failed. He was a man of strong emotions, freely expressed. I remember when he tried to teach me to box, which must have been in Larchmont, New York, in 1916 or early 1917, when I was seven years old. He put boxing gloves on me, a little pair he had bought for the purpose, and then put on his own boxing gloves, which he kept for occasional bouts with a punching bag, and took up a boxing stance. He urged me to come ahead and try to hit him, but I just collapsed with laughter at the very idea. I couldn't box with him, try as I might, but laughed so hard I fell down. He was saddened, obviously, but, with effort, refrained from blaming me for not coming up to his expectations.

Another memory is of the time Dad bought a box kite for me to fly. This was in Mahwah, New Jersey, when I was about five. It was the kind for which, these days, there is the familiar phrase, "some assembly required." He assembled and assembled and assembled, and still it wouldn't look like a box kite. When he finally got it into a box-like shape, I remember his desperate attempts to fix some kind of tail on it, the assembly apparently not including materials for that. When he got it completed, he tried to run with it against the breeze, holding the cord tight and hoping the kite would rise. Alas, it bounced on the ground and broke up into its constituent wooden strips and sheets of paper. I could see his dreams of his little boy holding the cord of a high-flying kite, sailing among the clouds—and then the dream, with the kite, crashing to earth with a splintering finality. He hugged me, and apologized for his ineptness at the boldly undertaken enterprise.

Another memory is not of my own recollection, but something my mother told me about, long after the event. When the Barnum & Bailey Circus used to give its exhibitions at the old Madison Square Garden, Dad used to be an enthusiastic circus-goer, as evinced by his essay, "The Circus." It was his cherished dream to introduce me, his eldest child, to the delights of a circus. At the time, we were living in Mahwah, and he was commuting between his work in New

York and his home, by way of the Erie Railroad. His earnings, for free-lance writings, of poems, essays, newspaper articles and interviews, and an occasional lecture, were minimal. One day he strained the family budget sufficiently to buy tickets for the circus, for himself and for me, and arranged somehow to have me handed over to him in New York (probably by my mother's mother, Ada Alden, who lived in New York). On the way in to the circus, he felt he could complete my enjoyment of the occasion by getting me an ice cream cone, spending, for the purpose, his last dime (aside from the coins carefully set aside for the subway or Hudson Tube to take us to the Jersey City terminal). Of course the ice cream fell off the cone, that was held in my youthful and inexpert hand. I cried, but the ice cream was irretrievable from that floor littered with straw, sawdust, and all sorts of dirt.

I can well imagine how deeply my Dad felt this frustration, striking at the heart of his effort to give the fullness of joy to his son. I, in my philosophical fashion, finished eating the bare cone when I had stopped crying, and then went on to enjoy the clowns, equestrians, freaks, animals, and gymnasts of the circus. But my mother remembered, and described to me, the bitterness with which my Dad bewailed his inability to provide me with that missing fragment of the circus experience.

Another memory, this time really my own recollection, is of a time when I thought Dad would be not only disappointed in me, but really enraged. At the dinner table, at our house in Mahwah, my mother asked Dad to pass the mustard. He said, "No, Aline, you don't want it." I burst out in a childish rage: "She does too want the mustard! Give it to her, you bad fool!" I awaited the thunder and lightning of his wrath, but, to my astonishment, he was pleased with me. He told me it was very right and brave of me to try to make sure that my mother got what she wanted, and apologized for not making clear the reason for his not passing the mustard as requested. It was, he explained, a kind of mustard (perhaps mixed with horseradish?) that my mother really didn't like. This was perhaps the first time that my Dad tried to teach me the lesson, basic to his philosophy, that a prime duty of a gentleman was to serve and protect his women-folk, and that bravery in their defense was among the highest virtues.

PENNIES

A few long-hoarded pennies in his hand,
Behold him stand;
A kilted Hedonist, perplexed and sad.
The joy that once he had
The first delight of ownership is fled.
He bows his little head.
Ah, cruel Time, to kill
That splendid thrill!

Then in his tear-dimmed eyes
New lights arise.
He drops his treasured pennies on the ground,
They roll and bound
And scattered, rest.
Now with what zest
He runs to find his errant wealth again!

So unto men
Doth God, depriving that He may bestow.
Fame, health and money go,
But that they may, new found, be newly sweet.
Yea, at His feet
Sit, waiting us, to their concealment bid,
All they, our lovers, whom His Love hath hid.

Lo, comfort blooms on pain, and peace on strife,
    And gain on loss.
What is the key to Everlasting Life?
    A blood-staind Cross.

—Joyce Kilmer

8. THE TIME I FROZE TO DEATH!
(Well, almost)

Speaking about how my Dad always wanted to give me the best time possible, and sometimes was deeply disappointed when he failed, I am reminded of the most spectacular failure he had in this respect. It was a cold, cold, snowy day in Mahwah—hard frozen snow on the ground and the sky like a bowl-cover of dark grey cloud. I must have been about four years old, which would make it the winter of 1912/13 or 1913/14. There's no way to check up on that, now, at the end of 1990! Dad had occasion to go down our hill, Airmount Road, to the general store that was our downtown center, to do some minor shopping. It must have been a Saturday, for him to be available for the errand and for the store to be open. Dad and Mother together bundled me up well for the journey: warm socks, boots, leggings over my socks and trousers, coat, wrap-around muffler, knitted woolly hat, and woolly mittens. I remember that I felt completely enclosed and immovable. They loaded me onto my little sled, a Flexible Flier, with firm injunctions to hold onto those steering handles, but not to steer. I don't remember the trip down the hill to the store, or whether I was taken into the store, but I do remember how, on the way back, I felt it harder and harder to hold on, and that I was afraid of rolling or sliding off the sled. Also, I felt colder and colder as Dad trudged up the hill, pulling the sled along, and every now and then reminding me to hold tight. By the time we reached our place, and he swung the sled and me into the front path and up to the steps to our front porch, I was absolutely immovable. I was also speechless. Dad picked me up and carried me into the house, where he and Mother worked over me with increasing concern and urgency. They peeled the clothes off me, picked me up, stiff as a board, and put me in the bathtub. Dad held my head up, while Mother ran the cold water into the tub to thaw me. I remember that, as I began to regain my ability to speak, I complained that the water was hot, but Mother explained to me that it was really cold water, just feeling hot because I was so cold. Dad, who had helped Grandad write the Johnson & Johnson first aid manual, knew well that cold water was then the standard prescription for thawing frozen portions of the

64

anatomy. I understand that, in later years, it was found that it was better to use hot, but not too hot, water for the purpose. Dad certainly felt that his effort to give me a good time, by taking me for a long ride on my sled, had utterly failed. But I learned a lesson: whenever I think I'm in danger of freezing, I make sure I move around a lot. I know what happens if I'm immobile in cold weather!

On quite another topic, I remember how Dad used to sing funny songs sometimes, when going around the house doing minor tasks, like putting a room in order or setting the table. The one song I remember -- not from his singing it, but from my mother's singing it, and telling me Dad made it up -- went to the tune of "Turkey in the Straw":

Oh, the old man sat by the side of a brook,
 A-readin' to hisself from a small green book,
When up jumped a cricket that was sittin' on the bank,
Sayin' 'Pardon me, Sir, but your taste is rank!'
Said the old man, 'Sir, this book which I read
Has many times served me in time of need.
I read it in the summer and I read it in the fall,
I read it in the winter and I SHALL READ IT ALL!'

I remember how Dad used to relish puns, and accidental confusions of similar-sounding words, like cricket and critic. He used to enjoy teasing me, like warning me to look out when eating a banana, because there was a B in it. That was when I was old enough to know how to spell, but not old enough to jump easily from the meaning of B to bee. I remember looking at the tiny brown specks to be found lined up in the deep inside of a banana, and asking if those were bees. By the time I understood the joke I had pretty well devoured the banana, with no stings.

Another time, I happily accepted from him a big round flat cookie, with a hole in the middle, but listened with concern as he warned me not to eat the hole. I dutifully nibbled around the edge of the hole, leaving that little rim, but he told me: "it's all right to eat the *rim* of the hole, I'm just telling you not to eat the *hole*! In fact, it's all right for you to eat the *whole* cookie." As usual with the victims of puns, I was more disgusted than amused, but I *did* relish the cookie.

THE SNOWMAN IN THE YARD

(For Thomas Augustine Daly)

The Judge's house has a splendid porch, with pillars and steps
      of stone,
    And the Judge has a lovely flowering hedge that came
      from across the seas;
In the Hales' garage you could put my house and everything I
      own,
    And the Hales have a lawn like an emerald and a row
      of poplar trees.

Now I have only a little house, and only a little lot,
    And only a few square yards of lawn, with dandelions
      starred;
But when Winter comes, I have something there that the Judge
      and the Hales have not,
    And it's better worth having than all their wealth—it's
      a snowman in the yard.

The Judge's money brings architects to make his mansion fair;
    The Hales have seven gardeners to make their roses
      grow;
The Judge can get his trees from Spain and France and
      everywhere,
    And raise his orchids under glass in the midst of all the
      snow.

But I have something no architect or gardener ever made,
    A thing that is made by the busy touch of little
      mittened hands;
And the Judge would give up his lonely estate, where the level
      snow is laid
    For the tiny house with the trampled yard, the yard
      where the snowman stands.

They say that after Adam and Eve were driven away in tears
    To toil and suffer their life-time through, because of
      the sin they sinned,
The Lord made Winter to punish them for half their exiled years,

66

To chill their blood with the snow, and pierce their
flesh with the icy wind.

But we who inherit the primal curse, and labour for our bread,
Have yet, thank God, the gift of Home, though Eden's
gate is barred:
And through the Winter's crystal veil, Love's roses blossom
red,
For him who lives in a house that has a snowman in
the yard.

—Joyce Kilmer

9. JOKES AND PLAY

Sometimes memories of my childhood come up in the most unexpected ways. A little over a week ago, for example, a joke of my father's, which I know about from my mother's having told me, turned up in a Sunday comic in The Washington Post, Hanna-Barbera's FLINTSTONES. In the first segment, Wilma tells Fred, "The garbage disposal makes a funny noise... What do you think is wrong, Fred?" Fred replies with the question, "Have you thrown ONIONS down the drain again?" and she answers "Yes.." as the sound "WAAAH" issues from under the sink. In the next segment, Fred opens the door under the sink, showing the resident pig, and says, "Well, that's your trouble right there! He hates onions."

Dad's elaborate plan of some seventy-five years ago (before the time of garbage disposals, I'm sure) was to buy from a farmer a very young and small pig, cage it under the sink, and feed it on food scraps from the dinner table. The payoff was to come, of course, when the pig had attained a reasonable size, and could be butchered and eaten.

For those who are younger than I, it might be well to explain, in this connection, that in many jurisdictions the various kinds of household waste had to be dealt with separately. Ashes, both coal and wood, were put in large covered metal cans; trash, (paper, metal, and glass), was put out in whatever container was found suitable; garbage, which was destined to be turned over to a pig farmer, had to be entirely composed of food scraps, with the strict avoidance of bones, glass, metal, or anything else that a pig shouldn't eat. I remember that my childhood ambition was to grow up to be an ash man or a trash man. I greatly admired the romantic figure they cut, as they stood on the step on the back of the truck careering up or down the hill, leapt off to seize the container of trash or ashes, leapt back to dump its contents into the truck, dropped the container by the roadside with, often, a loud clang, and charged off to the next stop. Often this adventurous career was given the musical accompaniment of whoops and hollers, to tell the driver of the truck when to stop, or when to drive on.

Dad's jokes were sometimes elaborate, like this one, and sometimes quite simple but persistent. I remember his regular

68

rule, often cited, that the kind of conversation designated as "drivel" was authorized only on one day of the year, "Drivel Day." If I, or any younger brother or sister, should start saying something that he considered "drivel," this rule would be called upon to quiet us. "Drivel Day" was June First, but there was an unwritten, unspoken rule that neither Dad nor Mother would ever remind any of us when Drivel Day actually occurred. Naturally, none of us children ever paid enough attention to the calendar to recognize Drivel Day when it arrived.

Dad used to enjoy talking to his children with mock ferocity. I remember asking my mother, one time, "What's a 'gutter-snapper'?" Naturally, my mother was momentarily bewildered, but I explained that Dad had called me that. After a little thought, she managed to straighten out my understanding. Dad had sometimes called me "a little guttersnipe," and sometimes "a young whipper-snapper." I had combined the terms. Dad's mock ferocity showed, also, when he grew a mustache, a part of his adoption of the part of a soldier in the period of his military training, and preparation for war. Noticing the effect of the mustache when he kissed his smaller children, such as Deborah and Michael, he called it his "baby-scratcher." I remember, by the way, how I used to appreciate the privilege of watching him shave, flourishing his straight razor, and wiping off the shaving soap from it with bits of toilet paper. When my own time came to shave, I used a straight razor, remembering how Dad used to do it.

Another childhood memory of my Dad is of his cigarette smoking. He used to enjoy rolling his own cigarettes, often using Bull Durham tobacco, that came in a little sack. I watched in fascination as he rolled the little square of paper around the tobacco, licked the edge to make it stick together, and then lit and smoked the cigarette. I remember, too, how when I used a little clay pipe to blow soap bubbles, Dad would inhale his cigarette smoke, and blow it through my pipe into the bubble. I greatly admired the effect of swirling smoke in the bubble. He used to smoke a pipe, too, sometimes, and I remember my mother's telling me how, one time, he was smoking his pipe as he waited for the train to pick him up at the station in Suffern, and put the pipe in his jacket pocket to

69

get on the train. Of course the jacket caught fire, and there was quite a commotion on the train till it was put out. I don't remember seeing the damaged jacket, but Mother said it was beyond repair.

Another memory of Dad's smoking is of the little rugs that used to come in cigar boxes, handsomely patterned little printed flannel cloths, just suited for use as rugs in doll houses. I used to contribute those rugs, given me by Dad, to the furnishing of the doll houses that my sisters Rose and Deborah and I played with. For that kind of playing, too, I remember with gratitude how Dad one time brought me, from New York, a complete miniature grocery store, its shelves stocked with tiny cardboard replicas of familiar cereal boxes, cans of meat and vegetables, boxes of tea and coffee, etc. What a delight it was to be able to play store with my little sisters, with such realistic equipment!

MAIN STREET

I like to look at the blossomy track of the moon upon the sea,
But it isn't half so fine a sight as Main Street used to be
When it all was covered over with a couple of feet of snow,
And over the crisp and radiant road the ringing sleighs would go.

Now, Main Street bordered with autumn leaves, it was a
      pleasant thing,
And its gutters were gay with dandelions early in the Spring;
I like to think of it white with frost or dusty in the heat,
Because I think it is humaner than any other street.

A city street that is busy and wide is ground by a thousand
      wheels,
And a burden of traffic on its breast is all it ever feels:
It is dully conscious of weight and speed and of work that
      never ends,
But it cannot be human like Main Street, and recognize its
      friends.

There were only about a hundred teams on Main Street in a day,
And twenty or thirty people, I guess, and some children out to
      play.
And there wasn't a wagon or buggy, or a man or a girl or a boy
That Main Street didn't remember, and somehow seem to enjoy.

The truck and the motor and trolley car and the elevated train
They make the weary city street reverberate with pain:
But there is yet an echo left deep down within my heart
Of the music the Main Street cobblestones made beneath a
      butcher's cart.

God be thanked for the Milky Way that runs across the sky,
That's the path my feet would tread whenever I have to die.
Some folks call it a Silver Sword, and some a Pearly Crown,
But the only thing I think it is, is Main Street, Heaventown.

                      —Joyce Kilmer

10. MY FIRST—AND LAST—LIE

This was my first attempt at fiction, and, though it was a sort of plagiarism, it succeeded surprisingly well. I was about five at the time, I think. We were living in Mahwah, and my mother had, for some reason that I don't now remember, to send me in to New York for her mother, Ada Alden, to take care of. This plan had been fully arranged over the telephone between my mother and her mother (Gran, to me), and Mother had put me on the train, Mahwah to Jersey City, to be met. I don't remember whether it was Gran or Aunt Constance, my mother's younger sister, who was to meet me.

All went quite according to schedule, and I arrived at Gran's and Grandaddy's apartment (Grandaddy, Henry Mills Alden, being off at work at Harper's Magazine, where he was Editor.) Somehow, it occurred to me to make an interesting story of my arrival—perhaps because Gran was a little unsure about why Mother had sent me to her. I began by assuring her that Dad was at home, adding, sobbing, that I wished that weren't so. Dad had stayed home from work that day, I told her, drinking hard, and getting violently drunk. He had started to come threateningly toward Mother and me, and we had rushed upstairs and taken refuge in the bathroom, which luckily could be locked. Mother had let me out by the bathroom window (I'm not sure whether I added details like a rope made of knotted towels), and with a hastily gathered handful of dollar bills and change, and told me how to buy my ticket to Jersey City and get on the train. I had run down the hill to the station, fortunately avoiding Dad's notice, and carefully followed those instructions, duly arriving at the meeting point. Gran listened in horrified fascination. When evening came, and Constance and Grandaddy arrived, they greeted my tale with considerable skepticism. With Grandaddy's experience as an editor, I guess he recognized fiction when he heard it. Anyway, the evening passed uneventfully, what with my early bedtime, and the next morning I was somehow returned to my home in Mahwah. I don't remember now whether Mother came to New York to get me, or I was put on a train for her to meet by a telephone arrangement like the first one.

In any case, there was some conversation between Gran

and Mother, and I don't know whether Gran had delicately questioned Mother about Dad's condition, or what, but somehow in their talk, by telephone or face to face, Mother learned the tale I had been telling. Nothing was said to me in Gran's presence (if they *were* face-to-face), but a good deal was said to me after the conversation! Mother immediately recognized key elements of my story as belonging to a sort of temperance tract in a little book I was fond of reading. The story was called "Little Jakey," and in it the German immigrant child of that name was abused, along with his mother, by a drunken father strongly resembling my fictitious Dad.

My mother believed, whenever possible, in following the Mikado's principle, to "let the punishment fit the crime." She therefore sentenced me to a certain term of days or weeks (maybe even months) without access to that particular favorite book, a volume in a series called, if I remember rightly, "Junior Classics." The particular volume, I remember clearly, was called "Childhood."

When Dad heard of my story, as I learned long afterward from Mother, she was surprised that he wasn't angry about my ornate and extravagant lie, or about the way in which I had painted him as a villain. "No," she told me, "what really enraged him was one particular remark you had made, about the early part of the adventure. You said, 'And I *told* Dad not to drink that second bottle of beer.' He resented the suggestion that a second bottle of beer would be too much for him!"

Well, neither Gran nor I had any judgment about a man's capacity for beer-drinking. My remark, lifted from Jakey, I suppose, was, if I may again turn to the Mikado, "merely corroborative detail, meant to add verisimilitude to an otherwise bald and unconvincing narrative."

Mother's method of discipline, like Dad's way of teaching by making me think things out, has given me a lasting memory. I'm not sure I ever lied again! And I still treasure the book with Little Jakey's story in it, though, I'm sorry to say, I can't find it right now among the thousands of books on our shelves. I have probably put it in "a safe place."

73

11. THEMES OF POETRY AND LIFE

As I reminisce about my father, my memories of him and his influence upon my development, I think, not only of how he influenced me when he and I were together, but how what I know of him, from his writings and from what has been written about him, has influenced my later life and character. I remember, for instance, how enthusiastic he was, both in speaking to me in the summer of 1917, before he sailed for France, and in the letters both to me and to my mother *from* France, about the prospect of my learning to serve Mass. In recent years I have thought of how happy he must be if he now knows that both my wife and I have been lay readers at Mass (as he was in the Episcopal Church), and have enjoyed the privilege, unthinkable in the Catholic Church of his day, of distributing the Eucharist.

In writing poems, I try to live up to the ideal expressed in his "Poets":

> Vain is the chiming of forgotten bells
> That the wind sways above a ruined shrine.
> Vainer his voice in whom no longer dwells
> Hunger that craves immortal Bread and Wine.
>
> Light songs we breathe that perish with our breath
> Out of our lips that have not kissed the rod.
> They do not live who have not tasted death.
> They only sing who are struck dumb by God.

The themes of my father's poetry were also the themes of his life. Kaleidoscopic as his nature seemed, since he threw himself wholly into the character of whatever part he was playing, like an actor on the stage, his spirit was true to three high ideals. Whatever he did, and whatever he wrote, from the time of his maturity, was an expression of his devotion to God, to country, and to all human beings, but especially his family.

His best known poem, "Trees," is an expression of another constant enthusiasm, that for nature, the outdoors, and plants, birds, and animals. Among people, his heart went out most warmly to those least appreciated by society—to bums,

74

drifters, hoboes, gypsies. One of my possessions is a deed to a plot of land (I forget where) that was to be devoted to the free use of gypsies. In western Pennsylvania there is a piece of land, dedicated to my father, offering camping opportunities to people in general, but especially to gypsies. And one of the Joyce Kilmer poems I most enjoy reading in public is "Dave Lilly," of whose hero Dad says admiringly, "He was shiftless and good-for-nothing, but he certainly could fish." I greatly enjoyed reading that poem, to tumultuous applause, at the celebration of the fiftieth anniversary of the dedication of the Joyce Kilmer Forest in North Carolina. That was in 1986, Dad's Centennial Year. That Forest is mountainous, and full of streams that must hold trout, and I'm sure many in the audience were ardent fishermen, like my Dad.

I remember, from our Mahwah days, seeing my Dad stride forth, dressed in rough outdoor clothes, such as Levis and a checked flannel shirt, either to fish in the Ramapo or one of its tributary streams, or just to walk in the wooded hills that are the Ramapos, mountains worn down by the thousands of years that they have stood in the snow and rain, wind and sunshine of the world. I remember, too, his doing rough countryman jobs about the yard, such as trimming branches from trees and bushes, and grubbing up stones from the yard. I watched in fascinated admiration as he took the larger stones down the hill to the end of the yard, and carefully fitted them each to each, building them into a sound, solid, free-standing stone wall. Like Robert Frost, he felt the importance of performing this task with full attention, so that whatever it is "that does not like a wall" would not come and topple the construction. I had good reason, next winter, to appreciate the solidity of that wall.

One day, when we had had a good snowfall, some of my friends came to join me in sledding down the convenient slope of our hill, from the path to our front door down to the level space at the end of the yard. We were all around five, six, and seven years old, and each had his or her own sled. I was quite new to coasting, as I had lived, up to then, mostly in New York City. Probably the sled was a Christmas present, being brought forth for my first opportunity to use it. We took turns, the half-dozen or so of us, running with our sleds down the hill to that path to our front door, and then throwing

ourselves down on the sleds, "belly-woppers," to coast as far
down the rest of the hill as we could. I was disappointed that
everyone else coasted faster and farther than I did. Then I
had a bright idea. I would start higher up, on the steeper part
of the hill that was just above the paved path, and see if that
wouldn't get me going faster and farther. Sure enough, it did.
I just flew down, at dazzling speed. As I approached the stone
wall, it occurred to me, a little late, that I didn't know how to
steer or brake! I slammed into that stone wall, and it didn't
budge an inch. I had my face up, looking right at it, and my
mouth smashed against a stone, splitting open. I remember a
little girl, one of my friends, crying and saying to her mother:
"Don't you slide down that hill, Momma, or your face will get
all red!" That was when I learned that peoples' skin could be
sewed just like their clothes. I got sewed and bandaged (I still
wouldn't know how to bandage a split lip!), and for a couple of
weeks or so I was on a completely liquid diet, taken through a
straw—or, more precisely, a glass tube obtained for the
occasion.

I didn't blame the wall, and I soon learned to steer the
Flexible Flier, and to use my foot-dragging capabilities to slow
or stop it. I didn't do so well, however, the next summer when
I tried to see how well it would slide on a mud slope. It started
down, sure enough, and then it stopped on the mud and I kept
on sliding, right off it into the mud. Not as bad as a stone
wall, but mud is grittier and more painful to scrape along than
you might expect.

Another outdoor task that I remember watching with
fascinated admiration was the cutting down of a tree. This
tree, a black birch, I think, was uncomfortably close to the
house, growing tall and stretching its roots in a way that
threatened our foundations. This was, I believe, the first time
I witnessed a team of men working together. A neighbor,
knowledgeable about the ways of trees, had told Dad of the
danger to the house from that tree, and had offered to help
take it down. As there were a couple of other trees not far
from it, he pointed out, it wouldn't be difficult or dangerous to
do the job, and the felled tree would be useful as firewood. So
he and Dad and another neighbor or two got together, one
climbing one tree and another climbing another, and they got
a stout rope coiled about the three trees, high up, so that when

the middle tree fell, it could be held and guided safely downward. I was, of course, obliged to watch from a safe distance. The men worked together, directed principally by the neighbor who had first proposed the project, trimming some branches from the tree selected for felling, and also trimming some bits from the branches of the other trees, so as to make sure of a clear path for laying the felled tree down. I can't remember now, some seventy-five years later, just how they went about the cutting, but it is my impression that some of the men were using hand saws, at least one man an axe, and that they had a big two-man saw, probably used only when the tree was down, to cut it into fireplace lengths. This was, I suppose, before mechanical saws were invented, and certainly before they became commonly available. I enjoyed noticing how my Dad, whom I had known up to then as the undisputed boss of the family (any differences between him and my mother being quite properly kept from me) took direction as a matter of course, and put in his own suggestions with deference to his more experienced partners in the task. It was exciting to watch the sawing and chopping, to hear the tree begin to creak and groan, and to hear the mens' shouts of alarm and warning when it started to fall in an unexpected direction. One man climbed one tree, and another another, and they pulled and hauled on the rope until they got the tree guided down as originally planned. Then Dad treated the team to one of his favorite drinks, I don't remember whether it was Jacob Ruppert's Knickerbocker Beer or Bass's Pale Ale. Either way, I always got to drain Dad's bottle.

I don't remember so vividly the cutting of the tree and its larger branches into logs, but I must have watched that, too, and perhaps even participated. What I *do* remember is how, after the tree had been reduced to manageable logs, Dad exercised the same skill and care he had used for the stone wall, in fitting the logs together, and piling them high, in a sound and solid woodpile, to wait for fireplace burning the next winter. And I remember, from New Brunswick visits and Mahwah and Larchmont living, what pleasure Dad took in stretching out, with his family around him, before a blazing and crackling fire.

77

APOLOGY (Excerpt)

(For Eleanor Rogers Cox)

For blows on the fort of evil
    That never shows a breach,
For terrible life-long races
    To a goal no foot can reach,
For reckless leaps into darkness
    With hands outstretched to a star,
There is jubilation in Heaven
    Where the great dead poets are.

There is joy over disappointment
    And delight in hopes that were vain.
Each poet is glad there was no cure
    To stop his lonely pain.
For nothing keeps a poet
    In his high singing mood
Like unappeasable hunger
    For unattainable food.
. . . . .
So not for the Rainbow taken
    And the magical White Bird snared
The poets sing grateful carols
    In the place to which they have fared;
But for their lifetime's passion,
    The quest that was fruitless and long,
They chorus their loud thanksgiving
    To the thorn-crowned Master of Song.

—Joyce Kilmer

VIGILS

Once I knelt in my shining mail
    Here by Thine altar all the night.
My heart beat proudly, my prayer rose loudly,
    But I looked to my armour to win the fight.

God, my lance was a broken reed,
    My mace a toy for a child's delight.
My helm is battered, my shield is shattered,
    I am stiff with wounds, and I lost the fight.

Low I kneel through the night again
    Hear my prayer, if my prayer be right!
Take for Thy token my proud heart broken.
    God, guide my arm! I go back to the fight.

—Aline Kilmer

THE POOR KING'S DAUGHTER

Had I been bred to spinning
I might have spun
From the cold break of day
To the night's beginning.
For my own slow weaving
I might have spun a thread
Fit for the robe of a king's daughter
Or a shroud to wind the dead.

But now my hands are idle.
Idly I go
With flamboys borne before me
To dance at birth or bridal.
And it takes twelve maidens
To robe me for my sleep,
And fifty gallant gentlemen
To guard my empty keep.

—Aline Kilmer

CITIZEN OF THE WORLD

No longer of Him be it said,
"He hath no place to lay His head."

In every land a constant lamp
Flames by His small and mighty camp.

There is no strange and distant place
That is not gladdened by His face.

And every nation kneels to hail
The Splendour shining through Its veil.

Cloistered beside the shouting street,
Silent, He calls me to His feet.

Imprisoned for His love of me,
He makes my spirit greatly free.

And through my lips that uttered sin
The King of Glory enters in.

—Joyce Kilmer

A BLUE VALENTINE

(For Aline)

Monsignore,
Right Reverend Bishop Valentinus,
Sometime of Interamna, which is called Ferni,
Now of the delightful Court of Heaven,
I respectfully salute you,
I genuflect,
And I kiss your episcopal ring.

It is not, Monsignore,
The fragrant memory of your holy life,
Nor that of your shining and glorious martyrdom,
Which causes me now to address you.
But since this is your august festival, Monsignore,
It seems appropriate to me to state
According to a venerable and agreeable custom,
That I love a beautiful lady.
Her eyes, Monsignore,
Are so blue that they put lovely little blue reflections
On everything that she looks at,
Such as a wall
Or the moon
Or my heart.

It is like the light coming through blue stained glass,
Yet not quite like it,
For the blueness is not transparent,
Only translucent.
Her soul's light shines through,
But her soul cannot be seen.
It is something elusive, whimsical, tender, wanton, infantile,
        wise
And noble.
She wears, Monsignore, a blue garment,
Made in the manner of the Japanese.
It is very blue—
I think that her eyes have made it more blue,
Sweetly staining it

As the pressure of her body has graciously given it form.
Loving her, Monsignore,
I love all her attributes;
But I believe
That even if I did not love her
I would love the blueness of her eyes,
And her blue garment, made in the manner of the Japanese.

Monsignore,
I have never before troubled you with a request.
The saints whose ears I chiefly worry with my pleas are the
        most exquisite and maternal Brigid,
Gallant Saint Stephen, who puts fire in my blood,
And your brother bishop, my patron,
The generous and jovial Saint Nicholas of Bari.
But, of your courtesy, Monsignore,
Do me this favour:
When you this morning make your way
To the Ivory Throne that bursts into bloom with roses because
        of her who sits upon it,
When you come to pay your devoirs to Our Lady,
I beg you, say to her:
"Madame, a poor poet, one of your singing servants yet on
        earth,
Has asked me to say that at this moment he is especially
        grateful to you
For wearing a blue gown."

—Joyce Kilmer

ROSES

I went to gather roses and twine them in a ring,
For I would make a posy, a posy for the King.
I got an hundred roses, the loveliest there be,
From the white rose vine and the pink rose bush and from the
           red rose tree.

But when I took my posy and laid it at His feet
I found He had His roses a million times more sweet.
There was a scarlet blossom upon each foot and hand,
And a great pink rose bloomed from His side for the healing of
           the land.

Now of this fair and awful King there is this marvel told,
That He wears a crown of linkéd thorns instead of one of gold.
Where there are thorns are roses, and I saw a line of red,
A little wreath of roses around His radiant head.

A red rose is His Sacred Heart, a white rose is His Face,
And His breath has turned the barren world to a rich and
           flowery place.
He is the Rose of Sharon, His gardener am I,
And I shall drink His fragrance in Heaven when I die.

—Joyce Kilmer

THE SINGING GIRL

There was a little maiden
  In blue and silver drest,
She sang to God in Heaven
  And God within her breast.

It flooded me with pleasure,
  It pierced me like a sword,
When this young maiden sang: "My soul
  Doth magnify the Lord."

The stars sing all together
  And hear the angels sing,
But they said they had never heard
  So beautiful a thing.

Saint Mary and Saint Joseph,
  And Saint Elizabeth,
Pray for us poets now
  And at the hour of death.

—Joyce Kilmer

EASTER

The air is like a butterfly
  With frail blue wings.
The happy earth looks at the sky
  And sings.

—Joyce Kilmer

12. OUR MAHWAH YARD AND NEIGHBORHOOD

Some of the things I am writing about are things I actually remember, but others are matters I was surely involved in, but only wish I could remember. One of these is the event Dad wrote about in his poem, "To a Blackbird and His Mate Who Died in the Spring." I can date that poem pretty well by a mention in Dad's letter to his mother, headed June 27, 1912. That was when I was three years old. The poem was dedicated to me, so I suppose Dad and I together must have found the pair of dead blackbirds, or else I had found them and told Dad about the tragedy. I treasure the poem, as a part of my relationship with my father, but deeply regret that I don't remember the blackbirds, their death, or the poem itself as of that early year in my life. Probably both Dad and Mother read it to me, but I remember it only from much later reading.

TO A BLACKBIRD AND HIS MATE WHO DIED
IN THE SPRING
(For Kenton)

An iron hand has stilled the throats
    That throbbed with loud and rhythmic glee
And dammed the flood of silver notes
    That drenched the world in melody.
The blosmy apple boughs are yearning
For their wild choristers' returning,
    But no swift wings flash through the tree.

Ye that were glad and fleet and strong,
    Shall Silence take you in her net?
And shall Death quell that radiant song
    Whose echo thrills the meadow yet?
Burst the frail web about you clinging
And charm Death's cruel heart with singing
    Till with strange tears his eyes are wet.

The scented morning of the year
    Is old and stale now ye are gone.
No friendly songs the children hear
    Among the bushes on the lawn.

When babies wander out a-Maying
Will ye, their bards, afar be straying?
      Unhymned by you, what is the dawn?

Nay, since ye loved ye cannot die.
      Above the stars is set your nest.
Through Heaven's fields ye sing and fly
      And in the trees of Heaven rest.
And little children in their dreaming
Shall see your soft black plumage gleaming
      And smile, by your clear music blest.

—Joyce Kilmer

Though I don't remember Dad's giving me this poem, or saying it or reading it to me, I am deeply grateful for the gift.

A 1913 letter, not more specifically dated, brings to mind something I do definitely remember. "The house," Dad writes, meaning the Mahwah house, "looks pretty well now. I dug a blind drain to keep surface water from running into the cellar." This would, I think, be in the summer of 1913, when I was four years old. I remember my bewilderment when Dad, with a hired ditch-digging assistant, engaged in the long and laborious process of digging a deep ditch near the house, around the corner from the front of the house to the side that faced down the hill. Like the tree-felling that I told about in another of my memories, this was a lesson in cooperation.

In the neighborhood group that aided Dad in cutting down that tree, and ensuring that it didn't damage the house or other trees in its fall, Dad and others acted in full subordination to the one neighbor who knew just how to do the job, each mentioning his own opinions, or shouting warnings when appropriate, but all acting in unison.

The ditch-digging was different, as I remember it, in that Dad was definitely the boss, and told the hired laborer just what to do, while working alongside of him. I remember his walking along beside the ditch, as it was being refilled with layers of stones, gravel, and (I think) sand, and reading directions from a printed sheet or leaflet, telling just how much of each should be used. The laborer was, I think, also a contractor of sorts, and had brought a wagonload or

88

truckload of these materials.

I don't remember now just what was done with the earth that had been removed from the ditch, but can make a good guess: big stones added to the stone wall, small stones put back in, where wanted, the clay subsoil used to fill in hollows in the hillside that Dad was trying to form into a lawn, and the topsoil, saved on some sort of tarpaulin, spread on top of the ditch, to be used as a flower garden for my mother's delight. I do remember the saving of the topsoil, that I definitely observed, and I remember that Dad explained to me, as well as to his hired helper, all that he was doing and the reasons for each step in the task.

It was in an upstairs bedroom of this house, which served as Mother's and Dad's bedroom and also as Dad's office, that Dad wrote "Trees," on February 2, 1913. I have his notebook with that title and date written down. The window looked out down a hill, on our well-wooded lawn—trees of many kinds, from mature trees to thin saplings: oaks, maples, black and white birches, and I don't know what else. My own poem, "Shadows and Light," gives a small child's impression of how the trees affected the inside of the house.

THE HOUSE WITH NOBODY IN IT

Whenever I walk to Suffern along the Erie track
I go by a poor old farmhouse with its shingles broken and
                                    black.
I suppose I've passed it a hundred times, but I always stop for
                                    a minute
And look at the house, the tragic house, the house with
                                    nobody in it.

I never have seen a haunted house, but I hear there are such
                                    things;
That they hold the talk of spirits, their mirth and sorrowings.
I know this house isn't haunted, and I wish it were, I do;
For it wouldn't be so lonely it if had a ghost or two.

This house on the road to Suffern needs a dozen panes of glass,
And somebody ought to weed the walk and take a scythe to the
                                    grass.
It needs new paint and shingles, and the vines should be
                                    trimmed and tied;
But what it needs the most of all is some people living inside.

If I had a lot of money and all my debts were paid
I'd put a gang of men to work with brush and saw and spade.
I'd buy that place and fix it up the way it used to be
And I'd find some people who wanted a home and give it to
                                    them free.

Now a new house standing empty, with staring window and
                                    door,
Looks idle, perhaps, and foolish, like a hat on its block in a
                                    store.
But there's nothing mournful about it, it cannot be sad and lone
For the lack of something within it that it has never known.

But a house that has done what a house should do, a house
                                    that has sheltered life,
That has put its loving wooden arms around a man and his wife,

A house that has echoed a baby's laugh and held up his
                              stumbling feet,
Is the saddest sight, when it's left alone, that ever your eyes
                              could meet.

So whenever I go to Suffern along the Erie track
I never go by the empty house without stopping and looking
                              back,
Yet it hurts me to look at the crumbling roof and the shutters
                              fallen apart,
For I can't help thinking the poor old house is a house with a
                              broken heart.

                                        —Joyce Kilmer

TREES

(For Mrs. Henry Mills Alden)

I think that I shall never see
A poem lovely as a tree.

A tree whose hungry mouth is prest
Against the earth's sweet flowing breast;

A tree that looks at God all day,
And lifts her leafy arms to pray;

A tree that may in Summer wear
A nest of robins in her hair;

Upon whose bosom snow has lain;
Who intimately lives with rain.

Poems are made by fools like me,
But only God can make a tree.

—Joyce Kilmer

Printed by permission of the copyright owner Jerry Vogel Music Co., Inc., New York, NY

SHADOWS AND LIGHT

It was late afternoon when I was put to bed,
And the sunlight slanted up from the low horizon
To our hillside house, painting a pale gold window
On our white wall—a window filled with dancing shadows
Of dark grey maple leaves.

I remember the leafy shadow-bough, lifting and lowering,
The leaves turned sideways, thin, or broadening to show as maple,
And all their sunny green turned dark and grey
Against the gilded wall.

I remember waking at night, to see brown rabbits dancing
On the moonlit lawn,
Their white tails flashing as they leapt and capered;
And on the wall a window of white moonlight
With a black leafy bough astir upon its brightness.

—Kenton Kilmer

THE TWELVE-FORTY-FIVE

Within the Jersey City shed
The engine coughs and shakes its head.
The smoke, a plume of red and white,
Waves madly in the face of night.
And now the grave incurious stars
Gleam on the groaning hurrying cars.
Against the kind and awful reign
Of darkness, this our angry train,
A noisy little rebel, pouts
Its brief defiance, flames and shouts—
And passes on, and leaves no trace.
For darkness holds its ancient place,
Serene and absolute, the king
Unchanged, of every living thing.
The houses lie obscure and still
In Rutherford and Carlton Hill.
Our lamps intensify the dark
Of slumbering Passaic Park.
And quiet holds the weary feet
That daily tramp through Prospect Street.
What though we clang and clank and roar
Through all Passaic's streets? No door
Will open, not an eye will see
Who this loud vagabond may be.
Upon my crimson cushioned seat,
In manufactured light and heat,
I feel unnatural and mean.
Outside the towns are cool and clean;
Curtained a while from sound and sight
They take God's gracious gift of night.
The stars are watchful over them.
On Clifton as on Bethlehem
The angels, leaning down the sky,
Shed peace and gentle dreams, and I—
I ride, I blasphemously ride
Through all the silent countryside.
The engine's shriek, the headlight's glare,
Pollute the still nocturnal air.

The cottages of Lake View sigh
And sleeping, frown as we pass by.
Why, even strident Patterson
Sleeps quietly as any nun.
Her foolish warring children keep
The grateful armistice of sleep.
For what tremendous errand's sake
Are we so blatantly awake?
What precious secret is our freight?
What king must be abroad so late?
Perhaps Death roams the hills to-night
And we rush forth to give him fight.
Or else, perhaps, we speed his way
To some remote unthinking prey.
Perhaps a woman writhes in pain
And listens—listens for the train!
The train, that like an angel sings,
The train, with healing on its wings.
Now "Hawthorne!" the conductor cries.
My neighbor starts and rubs his eyes.
He hurries yawning through the car
And steps out where the houses are.
This is the reason of our quest!
Not wantonly we break the rest
Of town and village, nor do we
Lightly profane night's sanctity.
What Love commands the train fulfills,
And beautiful upon the hills
Are these our feet of burnished steel.
Subtly and certainly I feel
That Glen Rock welcomes us to her
And silent Ridgewood seems to stir
And smile, because she knows the train
Has brought her children back again.
We carry people home—and so
God speeds us, wheresoe'er we go.
Hohokus, Waldwick, Allendale
Lift sleepy heads to give us hail.
In Ramsey, Mahwah, Suffern stand
Houses that wistfully demand

A father—son—some human thing
That this, the midnight train, may bring.
The trains that travel in the day
They hurry folks to work or play.
The midnight train is slow and old,
But of it let this thing be told,
To its high honour be it said,
It carries people home to bed.
My cottage lamp shines white and clear.
God bless the train that brought me here.

—Joyce Kilmer

13. RELIGIOUS PRINCIPLES AND
TEACHING WAYS

A guiding principle of my father's life seems to have been: "Whatsoever thy hand findeth to do, do it with all thy might." (Ecclesiastes 9, 10.) While he was a socialist, he felt obliged to be an atheist, bidding farewell to the allegiance he had held to the Protestant Episcopal Church, in which he had been a Lay Reader. Long after the passing of this phase, my mother told me that for a time, when she said her accustomed night prayers, she had to pray in silence and secrecy, lying in bed under the covers. Dad had forbidden her to pray, so, lying beside him in the bed, she prayed fervently for him, as well as for all other people and causes dear to her. For the time being, his hand had found the Marxist principle, "Religion is the opium of the people."

In my earliest memories of him, however, Dad was an enthusiastic Catholic convert, walking from Mahwah to Suffern, New York, every morning, to attend Mass and receive Communion before taking the express train to his work in New York. As my father, he was also my severe teacher in matters of faith and morals. Naturally, what I remember most vividly about this is the times when he and I were at odds about something. When I forgot to do something either parent had commanded, or forgot that they had forbidden some action, it was his firmly inculcated opinion that this forgetting was itself a serious sin of disobedience. I strongly (but quietly) disagreed. Now, as an experienced parent, I feel he had a point. It's just too easy for a child to slide subtly from forgetting a parent's commands to simply disregarding or dismissing them. Sometimes, strict and immediate obedience can make the difference between life and death.

Another memory is of the time Dad was helping me to memorize the Act of Contrition. When I came to the part called the "resolution of amendment," which goes: "and I firmly resolve, with the help of Thy grace, to confess my sins, to do penance, and to amend my life, Amen." I was running along confidently: "and I firmly resolve to confess my sins...," when Dad interrupted. He made me go back, over and over, telling me I had left out something important, but not telling me what it was. I was (quietly) furious when I found out that what I had omitted was the parenthetical phrase, "with the help of Thy grace." It was my six-year-old opinion that he should have just pointed out to me what the phrase was that I was leaving out. Now, however, I notice that I remember not only the phrase, but its importance in life. My resolve to amend my life becomes a part of my prayer only if I am asking for the help of God's grace in keeping that resolve. If he had just handed me the words, for rote recitation, the lesson might just have remained a matter of correct wording, and its deeper meaning might never have sunk in.

As in the matter of the hole in the cookie, and that of the "B" in the banana, so in this more serious affair, my Dad was the kind of teacher who makes a lesson memorable by forcing the pupil to think out the answer for himself. If you just tell me something, it may well slip out of my mind soon afterward, but if I have to work it out, I am likely to remember it forever. Maybe I'll resent that kind of teaching at the time, but I'll understand, later, both the learned answer, and the reason for the teaching method.

Another memory of a piety which I resented is that of a statue of Ste. Anne de Beaupré, which Dad had obtained when he lectured at the Canadian town of that name. When he brought the statue back after his trip—a little figure of silvery metal, on a small pedestal of the same metal—he had it duly blessed, probably at our parish church in Larchmont, and set it up on the mantelpiece in our living room. This was all very well, and I was happy to have it there, but what I resented was my Dad's decree that, whenever any of us faced the statue or passed in front of it, we must bow to it. Our front door opened on the living room, directly facing the fireplace, so that, by this decree, any time I came in the door I had to bow. Also, there were many occasions during every day when I had to pass from one end of the living room to the other. So this was one occasion on which I soon deliberately "forgot" to obey my father's command. Whether my mother, or even my father himself, managed to maintain the prescribed custom, I failed to notice. But I still wonder.

THE ROSARY

Not on the lute, or harp of many strings
    Shall all men praise the Master of all song.
    Our life is brief, one saith, and art is long;
And skilled must be the laureates of kings.
Silent, O lips that utter foolish things!
    Rest, awkward fingers striking all notes wrong!
    How from your toil shall issue, white and strong,
Music like that God's chosen poet sings?

There is one harp that any hand can play,
    And from its strings what harmonies arise!
There is one song that any mouth can say,—
    A song that lingers when all singing dies.
When on their beads our Mother's children pray,
    Immortal music charms the grateful skies.

—Joyce Kilmer

SANCTUARY

God has builded a house with a low lintel,
And in it He has put all manner of things.
Follow the clue through the mazes that lead to His door,
Look in! look in! see what is there for our finding.
Peace is there like a pearl, and rest and the end of seeking;
Light is there and refreshment, but there shall be more.
There we shall find for our use wide beautiful wings,
Ecstasy, solitude, space. And for those who have been too lonely
The love of friends, the warmth of a homely fire.
O never grieve again for the piteous ending
Of loveliness that could not be made to last!
There all bright passing beauty is held forever,
Free from the sense of tears, to be loved without regret.
There we shall find at their source music and love and laughter,
Colour and subtle fragrance and soft incredible textures;
Be sure we shall find what our weary hearts desire.
If we are tired of light there shall be velvet darkness
Falling across long fields, with stars, and a low voice calling,
Calling at last the word we thought would never be spoken.

But we, being hard and foolish and proud and mortal,
Are slow to bend and enter that humble portal.

—Aline Kilmer

ONE SHALL BE TAKEN AND THE OTHER LEFT

There is no Rachel any more
  And so it does not really matter.
    Leah alone is left, and she
    Goes her own way inscrutably.
    Soft-eyed she goes, content to scatter
Fine sand along a barren shore
Where there was sand enough before:
  Or from a well that has no water
    Raising a futile pitcher up
    Lifts to her lips an empty cup.
  Now she is Laban's only daughter:
There is no Rachel any more.

—Aline Kilmer

IF I HAD LOVED YOU MORE

If I had loved you more God would have had pity;
    He would never have left me here in this desolate place,
Left me to go on my knees to the door of Heaven
    Crying in vain for a little sight of your face.

How could I know that the earth would be dark without you?
    For you were always the lover and I the friend.
Now if there were any hope that I might find you
    I would go seeking you to the world's end.

"God is a jealous God. You have loved too wildly,
    You have loved too well!" one said.
I bowed my head, but my heart in scorn was crying
    That you whom I had not loved enough are dead.

I look on my heart and see it is hard and narrow,
    That my loves are slight and last but a little space.
But why do I go on my knees to the door of Heaven
    Crying for only a little sight of your face?

—Aline Kilmer

14. OUR IRISH AND IRISH-AMERICAN
FRIENDS AND RELATIONS

My recollections of my Dad would indeed be insufficient if
I failed to write about his enthusiasm for Ireland and the
Irish. A paragraph of his letter to my mother, from France,
dated April 21, 1918, is often referred to by writers who
wonder about Dad's claim to be "half Irish." It's on page 196
of Bob Holliday's collection of his prose works, the second
volume of the *Poems, Essays and Letters.*

"As to the matter of my own blood ... I did indeed tell a
good friend of mine who edits the book-review page of a
Chicago paper that I was 'half Irish.' But I have never been a
mathematician. The point I wished to make was that a large
percentage—which I have a perfect right to call half—of my
ancestry was Irish. For proof of this,you have only to refer to
the volumes containing the histories of my mother's and my
father's families. Of course I am an American, but one cannot
be pure American in blood unless one is an Indian. And I have
the good fortune to be able to claim, largely because of the
wise matrimonial selections of my progenitors on both sides,
Irish blood. And don't let anyone publish a statement
contrary to this."

Checking in *The Kilmer Family in America*, by Dad's
uncle the Rev. Charles Henry Kilmer, I find no apparently
Irish names among Dad's ancestors on the Kilmer side. An
aunt married someone named Finn—but that wouldn't affect
Dad's blood line! Granny's side seems more promising.
Kilburn is an English name, but Granny's mother, whose
maiden name was Ellen Smith, was the daughter of Hulda
Curtis. Smith can be, as in the case of Alfred E, the name of
an Irish-American, and I think Curtis, too, might be from
Ireland. In any case, Dad, in turn, made the "wise
matrimonial selection" of Aline Murray, whose ancestry
included such indisputably Irish names as Murphy, Barry,
and Donnelly. I'm sure Dad smiled upon my own "wise
matrimonial selection" of Frances Frieseke, daughter of Sadie
O'Bryan, and descendant of various other Irish or Irish-
American people, with such names as Donnelly (again!),
McCullough, and Duross. It was Caroline Giltinan Harlow,
Sadie O'Bryan Frieseke's cousin, and an Irish-American poet

103

well known to my Dad (as Caroline Giltinan, long before her marriage) who brought Frances and me together as young poets who might help one another through correspondence. My Aunt (by courtesy) Carol must get some of the credit for this "wise matrimonial selection"!

Dad's enthusiasm for the Irishness of the Sixty-ninth Regiment is well known, but long before America entered the war, he was enamored of Irish history, Irish legend and literature, and Irish and Irish-American poetry. Padraic Colum and his wife, Mary Colum the literary critic, were our good friends. I remember my mother speaking often of her admiration of the writing ability and literary taste of her friend, Molly Colum. One of my own happiest memories is of the time, while I was employed in the Library of Congress, that Padraic Colum gave a talk and reading there. After the talk, I went up to introduce myself to the speaker, remembering that he and my parents had been friends. "Kenton!" he shouted, holding his arms wide to embrace me. We had little opportunity for talk, but that moment is a glowing memory for me. For physical description, I remember well Theodore Maynard's story of an Irish countrywoman's remark. "And is that the great Padraic Colum? Why, he looks like something that would be lookin' at you out of a hole in the ground!" And for an indication of how many Irish people felt about Padraic Colum, I have the memory of a moment in Dublin. I asked directions of a policeman, and somehow the name of Padraic Colum came up, and I mentioned that I knew him, but wasn't sure whether he was living or dead. "Ah, glory be to God," he said, "he still lives!" Would that that were still true!

Dad used to frequent the company of Irish patriots, eager for Ireland to break free of British rule, but he also had some friends, still strongly Irish, who were for the modified autonomy called Home Rule. My mother once told me about such a friend, I don't know who it was, who was visiting us in Mahwah, and turned to me (about five years old at the time) and said, "Surely *you* wouldn't wish Ireland to become a republic!" "No, I wouldn't," I replied. Mother found it hard to keep from laughing, being, she told me, well aware that I wanted Ireland to be a kingdom, with myself as the king of it! But the friend went on to declare solemnly: "Even the

104

youngest of us must draw the line somewhere."

Other friends, besides the Colums, were the Donn Byrnes. Dad had made friends with Brian Donn Byrne in New York, when they were fellow-writers for various newspapers and magazines. In the summer of 1918, when Mother and I and the rest of us children were in Oak Bluffs, on Martha's Vineyard, Brian and Dolly Donn Byrne were in either that or a neighboring town, and we used to visit back and forth, my sister and brothers playing with their two children, Icca and McGumps (whose actual name, I think, was St. John, pronounced Sinjon). For some further years, before the Donn Byrnes moved to Ireland, they lived in Connecticut, not far from our Larchmont house, and we used to see them,now and then.

Dad much admired the poetry of Francis Carlin, and I treasure the poem that Francis Carlin wrote mourning Dad's death. I have been looking in vain for a copy of a poem by Francis Carlin that, to me, gives the essence of his Irishness. So I have to write it from memory.

The Two Nests
The wonder was on me in Curraghmagall
    When I was as tall as the height of your knee,
That a wren should be building a hole in a wall
    Instead of a nest in a tree.

And I still do be thinking it strange when I pass
    A pasture that has to be evenly ploughed,
That a lark should be building a nest in the grass
    Instead of a hole in a cloud.

Denis A. McCarthy, another Irish-American poet, wrote in a copy of his *Voices from Erin and Other Poems*:
To Joyce Kilmer

When I read your book, dear Joyce,
I can hear again your voice,
Hear your voice and see your smile—
Almost see your soul the while.

Wish I could make poems grow

105

Like those "Trees" of yours, you know,—
But I can't! Still here's to you!
And here's the best that I can do.

This verse and this book to Joyce Kilmer from his friend
Denis A. McCarthy.

An Irish friend much cherished by Dad was Seumas
MacManus. His *Donegal Fairy Stories* is a book I enjoyed and
read over and over in my childhood. I'm sorry to say its well-
worn condition is mostly my fault. It is inscribed: Michael
Barry Kilmer, with cordial greetings from Mariquita Páer
MacManus and Patricia Páer MacManus, March, 1916. Two
books by his deceased wife, Ethna Carbery, *The Four Winds
of Eirinn and The Passionate Hearts*, are inscribed by
Seumas MacManus of Donegal to Mr. Joyce Kilmer, January
1916.

Father Charles L. O'Donnell, CSC, was so well known as
the President of The University of Notre Dame for many
years, that his eminence as an Irish-American poet may be
insufficiently remembered. He was, however, President also,
for a period, of the Catholic Poetry Society of America. Like
Seumas MacManus, he celebrated in his writings not so much
Ireland in general as specifically Donegal. Some of his poems
are included in Dad's anthology, *Dreams and Images*, but I
feel that if Dad had known *this* poem by Father O'Donnell, he
would surely have included it:

A ROAD OF IRELAND

From Killybegs to Ardara is seven Irish miles,
    'Tis there the blackbirds whistle and the mating
    cuckoos call,
Beyond the fields the green sea glints, above the heaven smiles
    On all the white boreens that thread the glens of
    Donegal.

Along the roads what feet have passed, could they but tell the
    story
    Of ancient king and saint and bard, the roads have
    known them all;
Lough Derg, Doon Well, Glen Columcille, the names are yet a
    glory,

'Tis great ghosts in the gloaming remember Donegal.

The harbor slips of Killybegs glistened with Spanish sail
    The days Spain ventured round the world and held
        the half inthrall
And Ardara has writ her name in the proud books of the Gael,
    Though sleep has fallen on them now in dream-lit
Donegal.

Well, time will have its fling with dust, it is the changeless law.
    But this I like to think of, whatever may befall:
When she came up from Killybegs and he from Ardara
    My father met my mother on the road, in Donegal.

    As I mention Father O'Donnell, another memory of an amusing mistake comes up. As some readers may know, the full name of the food called "grits" is "hominy grits." In our family, when I was young, we used to have it as a boiled cereal for breakfast, and we called it "hominy." So one time, when Mother was seated at the piano, playing and singing a hymn, made from one of Father O'Donnell's poems, my little brother Michael, standing behind her, looking on and listening, asked, in great surprise: "What does that mean, 'He turned the stars to hominy'?" The line was, as Mother then had to explain through her laughter, "He tuned the stars to harmony."
    Another Irish-American poet who was close to both my father and my mother was Thomas Walsh, one of the founders of *The Commonweal*, and a noted poet, anthologist, and translator from the Spanish and other Hispanic languages. My copy of his *Hispanic Anthology* (published by the Hispanic Society of America, of which he was a Corresponding Member) is inscribed: for Aline in memory of dear Joyce, Thomas Walsh. Its dedication reads: To the memory of Joyce Kilmer, poet and hero, who earned a glorious grave near the river Ourcq, July 30, 1918, My Friend.
    Of Thomas Walsh's Irish Catholicism, I remember something told me by my mother. One time when he was visiting us in Larchmont, he happened to stay over a Sunday, and went to Mass with us. This, I think, was not long after Dad's death. He never knelt at the times of the Mass when kneeling is expected of the congregation, and my mother

explained to me that he had been wounded in the Spanish-American War—a bullet had lodged in his knee, and he was advised against having an operation to remove it. He walked well, but couldn't kneel. A friend and fellow-member of the congregation of St. Augustine's Church, having noticed his not kneeling, asked my mother, in the presence of us children, "Is he a Catholic?" Little Deborah, about four at the time, exclaimed: "Of course he's a Catholic! Wouldn't you know it to look at him?"

Irish (or Irish-American) Catholic priests were especially valued friends. Father James J. Daly, S.J. and Father Cornelius A. Shyne, S.J., both of whom he first knew at Campion College, Prairie-du-Chien, Wisconsin, were close to Dad, and remained dear to Mother and all of us children until their deaths. My brother Christopher, who died in 1984, had written, not long before, this poem addressed to Father Shyne:

TO CORNELIUS

If it should happen, comrade, that we meet
At this road's end, and I with weary feet
Sit down to rest before the Judgment Seat;
Will you, my friend, whom God will rise to greet—
As you are blest—tell Him I cannot stand,
And then extend your hand
In forceful prayer to let the Godhead know
I should be saved because I loved you so?

Nineteen of the letters in Bob Holliday's published collection are addressed to Father Daly. It was Father Shyne who helped my mother (and me) by working with Father Creedon to have me admitted, with a full scholarship, to Georgetown Preparatory School—admitted to the Eighth Grade, at the age of eleven, upon completion of the Fifth Grade! Both Father Daly and Father Shyne were notable for wit and humor, and the appreciation of humor.

Father Shyne, also, shared Dad's appreciation for Irish poetry. It was he who introduced me to the poetry of James Stephens, sending me the Stephens book called *A Poetry Recital*, inscribed: To Kenton, from Father C. A.Shyne, Sept.

108

28, 1927. This was, I think, to celebrate the fact that I was transferring from Holy Cross College, in Massachusetts, to St. Mary's College, St. Marys, Kansas, which was again a move, and a scholarship, that he had helped to engineer. Many of the poems in that book I soon committed to memory, and still know by heart.

Dad latched onto Father Francis P. Duffy, Chaplain of the Sixty-ninth Regiment, soon after entering the regiment, and Father Duffy remained a dear friend to us all until his death. I remember how pleased I was, as a boy, to be given a ride in Father Duffy's car, and to note that, while Governor Al Smith's licence plate read NY 1, Father Duffy's was NY 2. Another Irish-American priest friend was Father John Bernard Kelly, to be mentioned later in connection with my receipt of Dad's Croix de Guerre. He served for some years as Chaplain, and, I think, President, of the Catholic Writers' Guild. I remember in Mahwah, when I was very young, Father Kelly spent the night with us, and late at night I heard him stumbling up the stairs. Naturally, I thought he'd had too much to drink, but long afterward I decided I must have been doing him an injustice, when I learned that he was a victim of diabetes.

Eleanor Rogers Cox, much of whose poetry was based on Irish legend, was Dad's and Mother's friend, and several of her poems are included in Dad's anthology, *Dreams and Images*. She gave me, and inscribed to me, as a Christmas gift in 1918, both a volume of Scott's poems and Homer's *Iliad* in Alexander Pope's translation. At the time, grateful for the books and interested in reading them both. it didn't occur to me to think about her reason for choosing those particular books. Now, thinking back, I realize that Eleanor Rogers Cox, with poetic and sympathetic feeling, had realized the appropriateness of giving, to a nine-year-old boy whose poet father had recently died a heroic death in battle, books by two poets who most splendidly celebrated valor in war.

When Dad had decided to move the family from Mahwah to Larchmont, one inducement had been the friendship, and the practical arguments, of the poet Margaret Widdemer. To be out of the city, but close enough for easy and quick commuting, seemed ideal to Dad. Another inducement was that his friend Margaret Leamy, widow of the Irish M.P.

Edmund Leamy, lived in Larchmont. Edmund Leamy, as an Irish Member of the British Parliament, had worked with John Redmond and other patriots toward the establishment of Home Rule for Ireland. He was also a writer of fairy stories based on Irish legend, and including prose pictures of the Irish countryside. A poem of his, "Ireland," is included in *Dreams and Images*, along with several poems by his son, also named Edmund. The table of contents to the book has mixed up the names, calling the elder "Sir" Edmund, and his son "Edmund Leamy Senior." I remember vividly the time Dad had, trying to get that book ready for publication, choosing between a red cover and a blue cover, all in the moments he could have at home during his military training and preparation for sailing to France. I don't wonder that double error in the table of contents escaped his notice. Margaret Leamy, late in her life, wrote a memoir of the days of struggle against the British rule in Ireland, called "Parnell's Faithful Few." A play based upon her story was produced and had a brief Broadway run. I remember that Mrs. Leamy and Katherine Tynan Hinkson were good friends and frequent correspondents, in spite of distance. Mrs. Leamy and Mother, one day, were having tea together, with me as a silent listener and drinker of "cambric tea," when the postman brought a letter from Katherine Tynan, enclosing a recently written poem, and Mrs. Leamy read aloud to us both the letter and the poem. Mrs. Leamy was called Meg by Mother and her other friends, and in Mother's books about her children, where everyone appears under a different name, she is called "Nutmeg."

Another Irish-American poet much admired by both my father and my mother was Louise Imogen Guiney. Dad included four of her poems in his anthology, but I just don't know whether he knew her personally. I do know, however, that Mother was proud to count her among her friends, and that they wrote to each other sometimes. Mother also enjoyed reciting her poems, to me as well as to the audiences of her lectures.

Dad enjoyed a joyous friendship with Shaemas O'Sheel, a Chicagoan transplanted to New York. Writing poems based on Irish history and legend, he had changed his name from James Shields to the Gaelic forms of both names. They shared experiences, and exchanged advice, in the newspaper and magazine world of New York. I remember my difficulty with the spelling of Shaemas, since other friends of Dad's with what seemed the same name spelled it "Seumas." It was like the other puzzlement of my youthful brain, why the same stuff was always called ketchup, but sometimes labeled "Catsup." I asked Dad about that one, but don't know whether he had any answer. In the matter of names, my mother's teaching sufficed: "Anybody's name belongs to that person, and is to be spelled and pronounced as that person chooses." However he spelled his name, I know my father was enthusiastic about Shaemas O'Sheel's poetry, and relished the fact that he was steeped in Irish legend and history. Mother and Dad alike valued such poems as his "They Went Forth to Battle."

> They went forth to battle, but they always fell;
>   Their eyes were fixed above the sullen shields;
> Nobly they fought and bravely, but not well,
> And sank heart-wounded by a subtle spell.
>   They knew not fear that to the foeman yields,
>   They were not weak, as one who vainly wields
> A futile weapon, yet the sad scrolls tell
> How on the hard-fought field they always fell.
>
> It was a secret music that they heard,
>   A sad sweet plea for pity and for peace;
> And that which pierced the heart was but a word,
> Though the white breast was red-lipped where the sword
>   Pressed a fierce cruel kiss, to put surcease
>   On its hot thirst, but drank a hot increase.
> Ah, they by some strange troubling doubt were stirred,
> And died for hearing what no foeman heard.
>
> They went forth to battle but they always fell;
>   Their might was not the might of lifted spears;
> Over the battle-clamor came a spell
> Of troubling music, and they fought not well.
>   Their wreaths are willows and their tribute, tears;
>   Their names are old sad stories in men's ears;
> Yet they will scatter the red hordes of Hell,
> Who went to battle forth and always fell.

T. A. Daly, who chose not to use his full name of Thomas Augustine Daly, was another of Dad's cherished Irish-American friends. He wrote both serious verse, like the five poems Dad included in his anthology, and masterly light verse. The poetic conversation between him and Carolyn Wells, in which she mourns the fact that she had omitted him from her *Book of Humorous Verse*, and he gallantly accepts her apology, makes enjoyable reading and re-reading. Her poem is a ballade with the refrain, "Why did I leave out T. A. Daly?" His reply, skillfully parodying "Maryland, My Maryland," with the refrain, "Carolyn, my Carolyn," is a witty and complimentary reply from "the wild harp flung behind her," ending, "You didn't need, Carolyn, my carolin'!" When I was a freshman at Holy Cross College, in 1926-7, T.A. Daly came to give a talk, and I was privileged to have a talk with him, in which he expressed his affectionate memories and admiration of my father.

As I leaf through the table of contents of *Dreams and Images*, I am reminded of the many Irish and Irish-American poets Dad brought into our lives. Eleanor Donnelly differs from the others in that it's my wife who makes that connection. Eleanor Donnelly was, both to Caroline Giltinan and to my mother-in-law, Sadie O'Bryan, "Aunt Eleanor." Little did I think, when I studied her poetry in a graduate course in Catholic poetry at Georgetown under Theodore Maynard, that she was soon to become my great-aunt by marriage!

A little further on in the table of contents comes the name of Michael Earls, S.J. Like James J. Daly and Charles L. O'Donnell, he was an Irish Catholic poet-priest. On account of his affection for my father, Father Earls worked to get me a scholarship at Holy Cross College. I suppose my excellent academic record at Georgetown Prep helped!

Blanche Mary Kelly, like Mary Colum, was a friend and literary critic much admired by my mother. The name of Helen L. Moriarty also takes me back to college days. When I was a graduate student at The Catholic University of America, I boarded at a house owned by a Mrs. Moriarty, who told me proudly that her late husband's aunt (if I remember rightly) had a poem in Dad's anthology. And Speer Strahan, C.S.C., another Irish-American poet (or was he Scottish-American?)

included in the anthology, was my teacher in a course on Geoffrey Chaucer in the University. After I had left the University, he remained my friend by correspondence, up to his death as a military chaplain in the U.S. Army in the Philippines.

Pondering the changes that have occurred in Ireland since 1918, I feel confident that Dad would rejoice over the independence that the country has gained, but that he would mourn the division that still exists between Northern Ireland and the rest of the country, and the bitter conflict in the North. I rejoice in the memory of his poem, "Gates and Doors," being beamed over all Ireland, Christmas after Christmas, on the Irish radio; and I hope Dad, too, rejoiced to hear his poem ringing over the land he loved.

GATES AND DOORS

There was a gentle hostler
   (And blesséd be his name!)
He opened up the stable
   The night Our Lady came.
Our Lady and Saint Joseph,
   He gave them food and bed,
And Jesus Christ has given him
   A glory round his head.

So let the gate swing open
   However poor the yard,
Lest weary people visit you
   And find their passage barred;
Unlatch the door at midnight
   And let your lantern's glow
Shine out to guide the traveller's feet
   To you across the snow.

There was a courteous hostler
   (He is in Heaven to-night)
He held Our Lady's bridle
   And helped her to alight;
He spread clean straw before her
   Whereon she might lie down,
And Jesus Christ has given him
   an everlasting crown.

Unlock the door this evening
   And let your gate swing wide,
Let all who ask for shelter
   Come speedily inside.
What if your yard be narrow?
   What if your house be small?
There is a Guest is coming
   Will glorify it all.

There was a joyous hostler
   Who knelt on Christmas morn
Beside the radiant manger

Wherein his Lord was born.
His heart was full of laughter,
    His soul was full of bliss
When Jesus, on His Mother's lap,
    Gave him His hand to kiss.

Unbar your heart this evening
    And keep no stranger out,
Take from your soul's great portal
    The barrier of doubt.
To humble folk and weary
    Give hearty welcoming,
Your breast shall be to-morrow
    The cradle of a King.

—Joyce Kilmer

THE FOURTH SHEPHERD

(For Thomas Walsh)

On nights like this the huddled sheep
    Are like white clouds upon the grass,
And merry herdsmen guard their sleep,
    And chat and watch the big stars pass.

It is a pleasant thing to lie
    Upon the meadow on the hill
With kindly fellowship nearby
    Of sheep and men of gentle will.

I lean upon my broken crook
    And dream of sheep and grass and men—
O shameful eyes that cannot look
    On any honest thing again!

On bloody feet I clambered down
    And fled the wages of my sin,
I am the leavings of the town,
    And meanly serve its meanest inn.

I tramp the courtyard stones in grief,
    While sleep takes man and beast to her.
And every cloud is calling "Thief!"
    And every star calls "Murderer!"

The hand of God is sure and strong,
    Nor shall a man forever flee
The bitter punishment of wrong.
    The wrath of God is over me!

With ashen bread and wine of tears
    Shall I be solaced in my pain.
I wear through black and endless years
    Upon my brow the mark of Cain.

Poor vagabond, so old and mild,
    Will they not keep him for a night?
And She, a woman great with child,
    So frail and pitiful and white.

Good people, since the tavern door
    Is shut to you, come here instead.

116

See, I have cleansed my stable floor
    And piled fresh hay to make a bed.

Here is some milk and oaten cake.
    Lie down and sleep and rest you fair,
Nor fear, O simple folk, to take
    The bounty of a child of care.

On nights like this the huddled sheep—
    I never saw a night so fair.
How huge the sky is, and how deep!
    And how the planets flash and glare!

At dawn beside my drowsy flock
    What wingéd music I have heard!
But now the clouds with singing rock
    As if the sky were turning bird.

O blinding Light, O blinding Light!
    Burn through my heart with sweetest pain.
O flaming Song, most loudly bright,
    Consume away my deadly stain!

The stable glows against the sky,
    And who are these that throng the way?
My three old comrades hasten by
    And shining angels kneel and pray.

The door swings wide—I cannot go—
    I must and yet I dare not see.
Lord, who am I that I should know—
    Lord, God, be merciful to me!

O Whiteness, whiter than the fleece
    Of new-washed sheep on April sod!
O Breath of Life, O Prince of Peace,
    O Lamb of God, O Lamb of God!

—Joyce Kilmer

15. THE CROIX DE GUERRE

These are my memories of a time some seventy years ago, so it may be well for those interested to double-check by way of such resources as the New York Times Index for the period, and other periodicals when the dates of events have been ascertained.

When my father was at Camp Mills, Mineola, Long Island, expecting soon to sail for France with the Rainbow Division, he said a farewell to my mother and me. Kissing me goodbye, he said: "Don't let any other man kiss you until *I* come home and kiss you."

He was killed in action on July 30, 1918. The French Government, some time later, awarded him a posthumous Croix de Guerre, with a citation for acts of bravery.

When the Fighting Sixty-Ninth, after a prolonged stay in Europe for the post-war cleanup, returned to the United States, a grand reception and celebratory parade were planned. As a part of the celebration, my mother and I were, if I remember rightly, placed in the reviewing stand for the parade along Fifth Avenue. At a dramatic moment, either at a pause in the parade or at its conclusion, the ceremony of the presentation of the Croix de Guerre took place. The Citation, as I remember, was given by a representative of the French Government (civil or military, I don't remember) to a general in the United States Army, and the general then presented it to my mother. The medal itself was then passed similarly from the representative of the French to the American general, who pinned it on the lapel of my jacket. He and the spectators laughed when I shrank back from his kiss, probably thinking: "Typical American boy, can't stand to be kissed!" Only I knew that I was remembering my father's last words to me.

When all such ceremonies had been concluded, my mother and I, with my father's friend, Father John B. Kelly, were walking back through the city to wherever we were staying, when my mother suddenly looked down at me and asked: "Kenton, where's the medal?" I looked down at my lapel and could only answer feebly: "It must have fallen off." I remember bitterly Father Kelly's immediate remark: "Nobody home but the gas, and that's out." I thought then, and still think, that inadequate pinning on the part of the general was

118

the cause of that loss, and that I was not to be held responsible. In any case, some days or weeks later, probably through the efforts of our family friend, Father Francis P. Duffy, Chaplain of the Sixty-Ninth Regiment, a duplicate medal was obtained and presented in a private, but still formal, manner. I believe this ceremony took place in the Sixty-Ninth Armory, and I think a different officer did the pinning. This medal is the one I have given to the Lauinger Library of Georgetown University.

When my mother died, I was Executor of her estate, and thus took possession of the Citation. My memory fails me in this respect. I have given a photocopy to the Library. Either the original is somewhere in my house, or I may have given it to my brother Christopher, having the photocopy made for my own files. Christopher died in 1984, having served, in World War II, in our father's regiment, the Sixty-Ninth. One of his heirs *may* now have the original Citation.

The feeling that led to Dad's enlisting in the United States Army soon after our Declaration of War in the spring of 1917 may be traced to the rage he felt upon the torpedoing of the Lusitania on May 7, 1915. The poem, "The White Ships and the Red," was published in *The New York Times Magazine* on May 16, 1915. His feeling of outrage occasioned by this atrocity combined with his horror of the crimes against innocent civilian populations occasioned by the German invasions of Belgium and France, and made it inevitable that he would join enthusiastically in the American effort to repulse the German offensive.

The remaining poems in the following group effectively express Dad's feelings about war and peace.

I remember that when the United States Government (I forget what branch) asked my mother whether she wished Dad's body exhumed from the American Military Cemetery at Fère en Tardenois, and she consulted me about it, we both agreed that we should respect the sentiment Dad expressed in his lines:

There is on earth no worthier grave
To hold the bodies of the brave
Than this place of pain and pride
Where they nobly fought and nobly died.

His body, therefore, still lies in that Military Cemetery, and I was privileged to visit that grave several times, accompanied once by my brother Christopher, and one or more times (I forget) by my sister, Sister Michael. Frances, my wife, has also visited the grave with me.

THE WHITE SHIPS AND THE RED

With drooping sail and pennant
    That never a wind may reach,
They float in sunless waters
    Beside a sunless beach.
Their mighty masts and funnels
    Are white as driven snow,
And with a pallid radiance
    Their ghostly bulwarks glow.

Here is a Spanish galleon
    That once with gold was gay,
Here is a Roman trireme
    Whose hues outshone the day.
But Tyrian dyes have faded,
    And prows that once were bright
With rainbow stains wear only
    Death's livid, dreadful white.

White as the ice that clove her
    That unforgotten day,
Among her pallid sisters
    The grim *Titanic* lay.
And through the leagues above her
    She looked aghast, and said:
"What is this living ship that comes
    Where every ship is dead?"

The ghostly vessels trembled
    From ruined stern to prow;
What was this thing of terror
    That broke their vigil now?
Down through the startled ocean
    A mighty vessel came,
Not white, as all dead ships must be,
    But red, like living flame!

The pale green waves about her
    Were swiftly, strangely dyed,
By the great scarlet stream that flowed

From out her wounded side.
and all her decks were scarlet.
And all her shattered crew.
She sank among the white ghost ships
And stained them through and through.

The grim *Titanic* greeted her.
"And who art thou?" she said;
"Why dost thou join our ghostly fleet
Arrayed in living red?
We are the ships of sorrow
Who spend the weary night,
Until the dawn of Judgment Day
Obscure and still and white."

"Nay," said the scarlet visitor,
"Though I sink through the sea,
A ruined thing that was a ship,
I sink not as did ye.
For ye met with your destiny
By storm or rock or fight,
So through the lagging centuries
You wear your robes of white.

"But never crashing iceberg
Nor honest shot of foe,
Nor hidden reef has sent me
The way that I must go.
My wound that stains the waters,
My blood that is like flame,
Bear witness to a loathly deed,
A deed without a name.

"I went not forth to battle,
I carried friendly men,
The children played about my decks,
The women sang—and then—
And then—the sun blushed scarlet
And Heaven hid its face.
The world that God created
Became a shameful place!

"My wrong cries out for vengeance,
    The blow that sent me here
Was aimed in Hell. My dying scream
    Has reached Jehovah's ear.
Not all the seven oceans
    Shall wash away that stain;
Upon a brow that wears a crown
    I am the brand of Cain."

When God's great voice assembles
    The fleet on Judgment Day,
The ghosts of ruined ships will rise
    In sea and strait and bay.
Though they have lain for ages
    Beneath the changeless flood,
They shall be white as silver,
    But one—shall be like blood.

—Joyce Kilmer

KINGS

The Kings of the earth are men of might,
And cities are burned for their delight,
And the skies rain death in the silent night,
    And the hills belch death all day!

But the King of Heaven, Who made them all,
Is fair and gentle, and very small;
He lies in the straw, by the oxen's stall—
    Let them think of Him to-day!

                           —Joyce Kilmer

ROUGE BOUQUET

In a wood they call the Rouge Bouquet
There is a new-made grave to-day,
Built by never a spade nor pick
Yet covered with earth ten metres thick.
There lie many fighting men,
    Dead in their youthful prime,
Never to laugh nor love again
    Nor taste the Summertime.
For Death came flying through the air
And stopped his flight at the dugout stair,
Touched his prey and left them there,
    Clay to clay.
He hid their bodies stealthily
In the soil of the land they fought to free
    And fled away.
Now over the grave abrupt and clear
    Three volleys ring;
And perhaps their brave young spirits hear
    The bugle sing:
"Go to sleep!
Go to sleep!
Slumber well where the shell screamed and fell.
Let your rifles rest on the muddy floor,
You will not need them any more.
Danger's past;
Now at last,
Go to sleep!"

There is on earth no worthier grave
To hold the bodies of the brave
Than this place of pain and pride
Where they nobly fought and nobly died.
Never fear but in the skies
Saints and angels stand
Smiling with their holy eyes
    On this new-come band.
St. Michael's sword darts through the air
And touches the aureole on his hair
As he sees them stand saluting there,

His stalwart sons.
And Patrick, Brigid, Columkill
Rejoice that in veins of warriors still
    The Gael's blood runs.
And up to Heaven's doorway floats,
    From the wood called Rouge Bouquet,
A delicate cloud of buglenotes
    That softy say:
"Farewell!
Farewell!
Comrades true, born anew, peace to you!
Your souls shall be where the heroes are
And your memory shine like the morning star,
Brave and dear,
Shield us here.
Farewell!"

                          —Joyce Kilmer

THE PEACEMAKER

Upon his will he binds a radiant chain,
  For Freedom's sake he is no longer free.
  It is his task, the slave of Liberty,
With his own blood to wash away a stain.
That pain may cease, he yields his flesh to pain,
  To banish war, he must a warrior be.
  He dwells in Night, eternal Dawn to see,
And gladly dies, abundant life to gain.

What matters Death, if Freedom be not dead?
  No flags are fair, if Freedom's flag be furled.
Who fights for Freedom, goes with joyful tread
  To meet the fires of Hell against him hurled,
And has for captain Him whose thorn-wreathed head
  Smiles from the Cross upon a conquered world.

—Joyce Kilmer

PRAYER OF A SOLDIER

My shoulders ache beneath my pack
(Lie easier, Cross, upon His back).

I march with feet that burn and smart
(Tread, Holy Feet, upon my heart).

Men shout at me who may not speak
(They scourged Thy back and smote Thy cheek).

I may not lift a hand to clear
My eyes of salty drops that sear.

(Then shall my fickle soul forget
Thine Agony of Bloody Sweat?)

My rifle hand is stiff and numb
(From Thy pierced palm red rivers come).

Lord, Thou didst suffer more for me
Than all the hosts of land and sea.

So let me render back again
This millionth of Thy gift. Amen.

—Joyce Kilmer

MEMORIAL DAY

"Dulce et decorum est"

The bugle echoes shrill and sweet,
    But not of war it sings to-day.
The road is rhythmic with the feet
    Of men-at-arms who come to pray.

The roses blossom white and red
    On tombs where weary soldiers lie;
Flags wave above the honoured dead
    And martial music cleaves the sky.

Above their wreath-strewn graves we kneel,
    They kept the faith and fought the fight.
Through flying lead and crimson steel
    They plunged for Freedom and the Right.

May we, their grateful children, learn
    Their strength, who lie beneath this sod,
Who went through fire and death to earn
    At last the accolade of God.

In shining rank on rank arrayed
    They march, the legions of the Lord;
He is their Captain unafraid,
    The Prince of Peace...Who brought a sword.

—Joyce Kilmer

(ALFRED) JOYCE KILMER WAS BORN ON DECEMBER 6, 1886 AT THE HOME LOCATED AT 17 CODWISE AVENUE IN NEW BRUNSWICK, NEW JERSEY. THE HOUSE WAS PURCHASED BY THE STATE IN 1969. EARLIER CODWISE AVENUE WAS RENAMED JOYCE KILMER AVENUE.

JOYCE KILMER, TWO YEARS OF AGE

JOYCE KILMER, AGED BETWEEN FIVE AND
SIX MONTHS

131

JOYCE KILMER, FIVE YEARS OF AGE

CHILDISH VALENTINE TO HIS MOTHER, DRAWN AND COLOURED
BY HAND

RUTGERS COLLEGE

PREPARATORY · SCHOOL.

Report of *Joyce Kilmer*

YEAR.	1st	2d	3d	4th	Ex.	Av.
TARDY						
ABSENT						
DEPORTMENT	100	100	93	93		96
Arithmetic	85	95	88	95	85	90
Geography	91	77	83	76	70	79
Spelling	93	96	99	93	89	94
Grammar	94	97	99	96	99	97
Reading	87	88	-		88	88
Writing	91	91	92	93		92
Drawing		92	92	80		88

REPORT OF STANDING IN PREPARATORY
SCHOOL

JOYCE KILMER WAS GRADUATED FROM RUTGERS PREPARATORY SCHOOL IN 1904. HE STANDS IN THE CENTER OF THE TOP ROW IN A PHOTO TAKEN IN 1901 WHEN HE MOVED TO THE UPPER SCHOOL. COURTESY OF RUTGERS PREPARATORY SCHOOL.

ALINE MURRAY (KILMER), RUTGERS PREP, 1906

JOYCE KILMER IN THE CHARACTER OF *Sidney Carton*, WITH HIS MOTHER AS *Madame Lefarge* (DICKENS' "TALE OF TWO CITIES"), AT FANCY DRESS RECEPTION HELD BY DICKENS FELLOWSHIP, 1907

136

FRED KILMER, V.P. OF RESEARCH AND DEVELOPMENT
AT JOHNSON & JOHNSON

JOYCE KILMER, B.A. (COLUMBIA, '08)
Photograph by Underwood & Underwood, Taken
February 8, 1917

JOYCE KILMER (COLUMBIA, 1908) IN GRADUATION
GOWN, WITH HIS MOTHER

139

THE FAMOUS NEW BRUNSWICK WHITE OAK TREE WAS REDUCED TO A
MERE STUMP ON SEPTEMBER 18, 1963, AS STUDENTS, TEACHERS, AND
POETS WATCHED THE LIMBS REMOVED. JOYCE KILMER DISCOVERED THE
TREE IN 1904 WHILE A STUDENT AT RUTGERS PREPARATORY SCHOOL. A
SMALL, NEW WHITE OAK TREE WAS PLANTED IN DECEMBER, 1986 NEXT
TO THE RUTGERS LABOR EDUCATION CENTER.

JOYCE KILMER AND HIS MOTHER ON RETURN TRIP
FROM ENGLAND, 1914

JOYCE KILMER WITH A GROUP TO FIGHT A MAHWAH, N.J. BRUSH FIRE IN MAY, 1916.

MOTHER OF SERGEANT JOYCE KILMER, 1917. TAKEN AT
JOYCE'S REQUEST

143

PRIVATE JOYCE KILMER, JUST AFTER HIS TRANSFER
TO THE 165TH (69TH) REGIMENT

POSTCARD SENT FROM FRANCE. INSCRIPTION ON REVERSE SIDE: "YOU MUST GET THIS SONG. IT IS TREMENDOUSLY POPULAR AMONG THE FRENCH AND AMERICAN SOLDIERS. I HOPE TO HEAR YOU SING IT BEFORE LONG"

POSTCARD PHOTOGRAPH OF SERGEANT JOYCE KILMER, SENT FROM FRANCE

145

ALINE KILMER, 1919

146

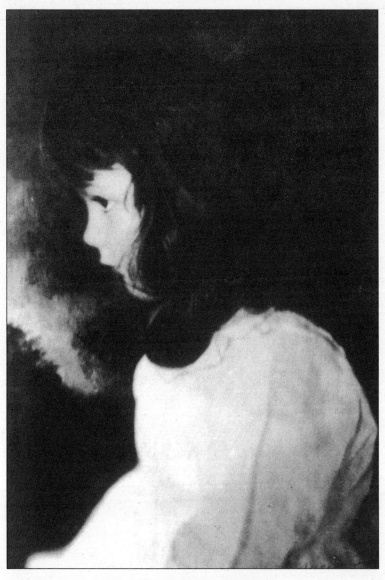

ROSE KILBURN KILMER (ROSAMONDE)
BORN NOVEMBER 15, 1912
DIED SEPTEMBER 9, 1917

ALINE KILMER AND CHILDREN, WALNUT AVENUE HOUSE IN
LARCHMONT, NY ABOUT 1920. CHILDREN: KENTON, MICHAEL,
CHRISTOPHER, DEBORAH (ROSE DIED IN 1917).

KENTON KILMER, ABOUT 1920.

PORTRAIT OF JOYCE KILMER © 1981, MIRIAM A. KILMER

KENTON KILMER © 1992, MIRIAM A. KILMER

HIGHLAND PARK IS ONLY 1½ MILES FROM THE KILMER HOUSE IN NEW BRUNSWICK, N.J. A WORLD WAR I DOUGHBOY STATUE IS LOCATED WHERE JOYCE KILMER WOULD WALK TO THE ABOVE *FORMER* HOTEL. THE DOUGHBOY STANDS NEXT TO A CUT DOWN TREE.

152

16. JOYCE KILMER'S LETTERS TO HIS MOTHER, ANNIE KILBURN KILMER*

Dear Brat is explained by Joyce Kilmer's mother. (Alfred) Joyce Kilmer was born on December 6, 1886.

LETTERS

A word of explanation may be of interest as to the heading of these letters, which I have not cared to change. Even before my son outgrew me in stature, it was his custom to treat me with a playful condescension, as though I were his junior. He always addressed me as "Infant," and every letter began, "Dear Brat," using the word in the old English sense of "Child."

"Oh Israel! Oh!household of the Lord!
Oh Abraham's *brats*, Oh brood of blessed seed!"
—Gascoigne.

And Aldrich says in one of his poems—
"The brat that tugged at his mother's gown."

He had a habit of neglecting to put a date on his letters, hence many that have appeared are without date.

———

1906

MRS. KILBURN-KILMER—I will be delighted to have you attend service at 5 in the church today.

Do the responses loudly, and wait for me after church. Hooray!

I remain, Yours Scornfully,
ALF. J. KILBURN-KILMER.
Official representative of the Kilburn familee.

———

(The foregoing was an invitation to hear him read the service in Christ Church when he was lay reader.—A.K.K.)

*Pages 154 through 261 have been reproduced from Annie Kilburn Kilmer's *Memories of My Son Sergeant Joyce Kilmer*, ©1920.

153

ADMIRABLE BRAT—The coupé for this evening has been ordered, and will come at twenty minutes before eight. Six large juicy white pinks for you, six pink ones for the small Murray child, and some cheap and ridiculous flowers for Sflager have been ordered and will arrive opportunely. Wortman and his female will be here delightedly at half past five, so will I and the despised Constance.

Behold your Glee Club tickets! Murph asked after your health tearfully. I lunched today at Viereck's luxuriously with Raymond Ashley, Delta U. Rutgers '03, now an instructor at Yale. He wants to meet you. Hooray!

Stover will leave the blue and gold ribbon here this afternoon.

Wash your face, pull up your socks, and put a minute red rose in your hair. You will look cute! You must dance tonight! Hooray!

I now go to help Mrs. Payson and Gies fix up the Delta U. House for the dance, and to go thence to Metuchen.

JOYCE KILMER.

1907

DEAR BRAT—I am not soused, but writing on my knee in the train, which renders my chirography slightly irregular.

Please bring my two Physics note books. They are in the top drawer of the reception room desk. I *must* have them.

I will appear for luncheon Tuesday at 12.15.

Yours affectionately, JOYCE.

Lake View House, Gale, N. Y., June 10, 1908

DEAR BRAT—We stayed over at the Manhattan last night, and took the 8:30 from the Grand Central this morning—the Empire State Express. We arrived here at about 8. It is a nice place, the table is fine, and our bungalow is very nice.

In the excitement of our escape, neither Aline nor I bade goodbye to my father or Mr. Alden. Please explain it to my father. And please send me my fairy story—which is in pencil on paper in the dining room bookcase, also my tooth brush, and a package of typewriting paper I left in Schussler's, and some note paper.

How did the Socialist meeting come off?

Be a good child, and write nice letters. You certainly looked cute last night. Aline sends love to you and my father.

Yours affectionately, JOYCE.

_____

(This letter was written the day after his marriage. This and the other letters from Gale were written while on his wedding trip.—A.K.K.)

———

Lake View House, Gale, N. Y., June 11, 1908

DEAR BRAT—I have not heard from you yet, but I nevertheless write. My trunk has not come yet, so I have no addressed envelopes.

We saw a deer last night, tonight a doe and a fawn. This is a delightful place—altitude about 2500, forests all around the house, a nice lake. We have a row boat for our own private use. The bungalow is very nice—one good-sized room, with a wood stove and a broad piazza with chairs and a hammock and a desk. The food is excellent—think of brook trout and wheat cakes for breakfast!

Well, be a good child, and write soon.

Yours affectionately, JOYCE.

155

Lake View House, Gale, N. Y., June 12, 1908

DEAR BRAT—My trunk came today, so I have stamped envelopes to write to you. I have not heard from you yet. Vile infant, I thought you were going to write daily!

Mrs. Corbin has sent me a hammock—which reminds me! For Heaven's sake, send me my typewriter! I meant to send out swarms of manuscript this summer, but I cannot do so without my typewriter. If with it you will put my tooth brush and writing paper and a few of my flannel shirts, and send them to me express collect, I will be much obliged.

I hope you and my father are well. I will write to him tomorrow.

Yours affectionately, JOYCE.

Lake View House, Gale, N. Y., 1908

DEAR BRAT—I have received one letter from you and have written daily. Today came a rather irate letter from my father.

However, it is a fine day. But I wish I had secured my bathing suit before I left. Still, I manage to swim occasionally, wearing Mr. Gale's overalls.

Letters only take about a day to get here, but they take the Deuce of a while to leave. One mail a day at 5:30 P. M. goes to the station at Childwold from the post office here, which is a little store kept by Mr. Gale for the convenience of the guides, hunters and fishermen. Then the mail goes out from Childwold sometime next day.

Well, don't forget to send my typewriter. Remember me to Ida. With love for you and my father, I remain,

Yours affectionately, JOYCE.

156

Gale, 1908

DEAR BRAT—I was glad to get your letter about the reception at Mrs. Payson's—it was an amiable letter from an amiable infant. Also I was glad to receive the *Home News* and *Times*—the wedding certainly had a large write-up.

Deer are numerous here; when we were out on the lake last night we saw four. Also we have brook trout every day.

It's rather hot, and I think there will be a storm. It's always cool evenings here.

By the way, will you please send me a bathing suit? I forgot to get one—36 in. chest. Just trunks and a shirt will do. Send me the bill and I'll pay you by next mail. These mosquitoes bite vilely before a storm.

Yours affectionately, JOYCE.

Gale, N. Y., 1908

DEAR BRAT—I hope you have a large time on board the *Mesaba*. Wear a good deal of red, and raise Heck with all the crew from the skipper to the stokers. Cut out any other skirt that dares to flare alongside. Wash your face daily and you will overcome all rivals.

As I write there is as much moisture about me as there will be about you when you read. It is raining—the mountain we live on is cloud-covered and the forest is dripping and the lake is as usual considerably moist! Well, enjoy yourself, Brat!

Yours affectionately, JOYCE.

157

Gale, N. Y.

DEAR BRAT—By the time you get this you will be at the coast of England. I hope they have sense enough to send this letter down to the boat. Aline wishes a rubber stemmed dark briar pipe brought her from England. She wishes the wood to be thick and flawless, the stem to be of hard rubber, curved. She is too shy to ask for it herself, so I do so.

If in the course of your wanderings you happen to see Mr. Bailey, you might tell him about the poem I wrote for him, and tell him I'll send him a copy sometime.

Yours affectionately, JOYCE.

Gale, N. Y., 1908

DEAR BRAT—I don't know what part of England you will be in when you get this letter. Cleveland is dead. Taft and Sherman are nominated for President and Vice-President on the Republican ticket, and Aline's bathing suit has come.

I ordered your present today. It is to come from London, and is something I selected long ago, but could not then buy. I think you will like it; you will get it on your birthday. It is very Red! and otherwise also amiable.

I hear from my father occasionally. He appears to be existing excellently. Constance is at Lake George. The bathing suit you sent me is fine. We go bathing a good deal, as the water is warm and the bank gently sloping, so that you go several rods before the water reaches your shoulders.

Well, I must catch this mail, so I can't write any more now. Be a good infant.

Yours affectionately, JOYCE.

158

Gale, N. Y., 1908

DEAR BRAT—I have not yet heard from you, but I have sent several letters which I hope you received when you landed. As to your present—but I suppose you will get this letter before your birthday. The large present is the one I wanted to give you, but my father insisted on having it come from him too, and paying for part of it. I hope you like it; in fact, I know you will.

Do you think I will look amiable with a beard? I am horribly sunburned, and my razor was dull, and Aline, to escape being beaten with an axe whenever I shaved and hurt myself, at length regretfully said I could stop shaving until we went to Morristown. So I have stopped shaving. I am a dull brick-red in color, and since I have ceased shaving, patches of dark green hair have appeared at intervals on my chin. It is a pleasant sight. However, I have gained in weight and am in fact becoming very fat.

I received a letter from Morristown today about my work, telling me the names of the books I was to use, and so forth.

Remember me to all my friends you see. I will send you, before long, a copy of "Rose Grey" to send Mr. Bailey, or to give him, if you see him.

I am at work on a play now—a sort of a morality, like Every Man, but laid in modern times—modelled on Maeterlinck and Fiona Macleod.

Yours affectionately, JOYCE.

Lake View House, Gale, N. Y., July 10, 1908

DEAR BRAT—Being the son of my father, I forgot to put the Delta U. employment agency pamphlet in the last letter, in which I said it was enclosed. However, I enclose it now, and a newspaper clipping about our little Howard. By the way, did he graduate this June? Your letters were suspiciously silent about his graduation.

Here is a translation of a Latin love song which I have made. I hope you appreciate it.

> If you were a buttered chameleon
> And I were a spoonful of tea,
> And I should attract your attention
> And you sate your hunger on me,
>
> And I should give you indigestion
> And you die all over the floor,
> Should I go to Heaven, I wonder,
> Or merely exist no more?

Since last writing to you, I have received a letter from a fellow named Compton I knew at the University. His aunt (whom I met at the class day dance) is interested (as a stockholder) in a private school for boys in Plainfield, and secured for me the position of English master at $700 per annum. Of course, I wouldn't take it—pay too small, and no prestige—but it's nice to have these offers.

Well, I must catch this mail. Your amiable letters from the boat came today. Wear red and wash your face daily and you'll be all right.

Yours affectionately, JOYCE.

Gale, N. Y., 1908

DEAR BRAT—I have had only one letter from you since you left America—the one written when you were about to land. However, my father sent us a swarm of amiable young letters you had sent him, and I enjoyed them very much. You evidently had a large time aboard the ship. The letters describing the journey to High Kilburn—the messenger boy and Salvation Army girl episode—reminded me of Sterne—pretty good! But then you have acquired a certain knack of description from my instructions.

Aline is making raspberry jam. Pray for it, for it is in tribulation. It is being made on a wood fire, which occasionally blazes up, and occasionally goes out. We picked the berries this morning. She is going to put up some blackberries and some huckleberries, and has expressed insane desires to make mixtures after your manner. I curb her with difficulty and an axe.

However, I enclose "Lizette," for you to give or send to Mr. Bailey, and some more poetry for your delectation and improvement.

We would like to hear from you more often!! Cut out raising Heck awhile and chronicle your adventures for us!

Yours affectionately, JOYCE.

DEAR BRAT—This will probably be the last letter I will write you from Gale, for we are going to New Brunswick to visit at 147 for a week or so. As soon as we find a cheap mansion in Morristown, and get it furnished, we will probably move in.

For a long time we did not hear from you, but I continued to fire off letters. A day or so ago came a pipe, two letters, and a swarm of amiable post-cards, one of which had the nerve to curse me bitterly for not writing! It is curious that you should be visiting places where Sterne had lived, just when I was reading the letters you wrote to my father (which he sent me) and noticing their strong flavor of Sterne. You should read "The Sentimental Journey." You would enjoy it, I know. It's not so well known as some of Sterne's stuff, but I like it best. The pipe is amiable—I never saw one of those patent pipes I liked so well. It didn't burn my tongue when I "broke it in," as most pipes do, and I am with difficulty restrained from smoking it at meals and when in swimming. Much obliged!

However, I wonder how we will get along when visiting my parent in New Brunswick. I think to make myself agreeable, I will demand booze with all my meals, will read the *Smart Set* aloud, and invite Seaumas O'Shiel out for a visit.

Don't forget to give or send "Lizette" to Mr. Bailey.

I am much obliged for your letters, all of which I guess I've received, and wish they were more numerous!

I enclose some poetry.

Your affectionate son, JOYCE.

162

NAIADS

In the sunlight softly showing,
Maiden forms are whitely glowing
Magic maidens wrapped in gleaming,
Robes of light are streaming, streaming
Over rocks and mosses splashing,
Ever singing, ever dashing
Silver clouds on high!

And their haunting, ceaseless singing
Through my maddened brain is ringing,
For they sing not love nor laughter,
Know not life nor what comes after.
Only know the poet's pleasure,
For they win his dearest treasure,
Make sweet sounds and die!

New Brunswick, N. J., Aug. 4, 1908

DEAR BRAT—Many large returns of today. I will osculate and smite you the requisite 26 times when I see you!

I received an amiable letter from you yesterday. God have Mercy on Harold, and on all Christian souls. Deal gently, good man-destroying infant, with the simple Yorkshire lads. They are but mortal. However, you seem to revel in the carnage. Did you send my poem about "Lizette" to Mr. Bailey?

I hope you liked your birthday present. I have another one for you, which I will give you when you return, as I can't post it conveniently. It is red, but further I will not state.

I am writing a series of articles for *Red Cross Notes* on the "Psychology of Advertising." My father is at the dinner of the Directors of Johnson & Johnson at present.

Aline is experimenting in cookery. She has made biscuits, cookies and corn pudding, and is going to put up some peaches.

Yours enthusiastically affectionately, JOYCE.

DEAR BRAT—Hail! But do not, for the love of Heaven, carry that stick! You are expected immediately in Morristown—let New Brunswick go to the Deuce! We have an amiable young house, and a room for you, red and white, as much as possible. You are expected to stay here for some years, and if you attempt to leave, your stick will be broken into seven pieces.

Cold weather. However, you must visit the school. I have in all about one hundred pupils.

The pipe you gave me is broken in now, and is delectable.

In the Morristown Local of the Socialist Party we have one doctor, one aristocrat (Arrowsmith, late of Seabury & Johnson) and the local Baptist minister.

Hoping immediately to see you, I am,

Yours affectionately, JOYCE.

1909

DEAR BRAT—Congratulations on the Dickens book from Kain!

We have made a window seat in the dining room, and covered it with the red piano cover. The blue portières are hung in the dining room alcove, and some of the lace curtains upstairs.

I have finished my fairy story that I started last summer, and written my bullfight story. I have to deliver an address on the 29th on "The College Man and Religion." It is a large opportunity. The scene is to be South St. Presbyterian Church. By gad I will give them Heck! I may be mobbed, but I will have an enjoyable evening.

We were naturally disappointed that you didn't come Thursday. Come out this Thursday, or have your face stepped on. Yours affectionately, JOYCE.

DEAR BRAT—Much obliged for the *Post*, with picture of Deacon Hill shrinking from a bath, for the *Home News* and for the candy. The candy was darn good—I never ate any grape fruit peel candied before, and like it much better than candied orange peel.

We have an excellent chance for renting the house.

Also much obliged for the *Smart Set*. It was a very good number. I suppose you have seen my poem in the current number of *Moods*. I have about a dozen mss. out now, and hope to place some soon. Please tell my father that his mss. is corrected, and will leave here tomorrow, with a batch of stuff for *Red Cross Notes*.

I have sent in my name to Pratt's Agency for a new job next year to be on the safe side, but Miss Brown says I'll probably be reelected here. However, I want $200.00 more a year. I am going to try for a job with some N. Y. concern anyway, like the *Town and Country* one I nearly landed.

Well, be a good brat. I am glad to hear you are in a proper state of mind now. Telephone at your convenience! Preferably evenings.

Hoping soon to see you, I am, Yours affectionately, JOYCE.

Thursday, 1909

HELLO BRAT!—I hear you telephoned to me this morning. I regret that I was sweetly sleeping at the time. I did not have all my evening clothes, and Aline was weary, so we stayed home and rested, retiring early.

This afternoon I worked some, and read some *Nicholas Nickleby* aloud to the children. It is a fine day. I will call you up today, Thursday, but I suppose this letter won't reach you till after I have telephoned you.

Be a good child, wash your face daily.

My poem is half done! and I have just sent off my Psychology note to Prof. Woodworth.

Yours affectionately, JOYCE.

DEAR BRAT—The doctor came today and, after examining Kenton, said no further operation was necessary. This is in many respects fortunate.

Will you please give Netty a quarter and say I sent it. I'll pay you Friday when you're here. I forgot to tip her yesterday, and I can't send a quarter by mail easily.

It rained just enough to keep down the dust yesterday, and we did not get wet. Kenton is well, and occasionally speaks of his visit to New Brunswick with much enthusiasm.

We had a darn good time in New Brunswick.

The Breeces are astonished at my resplendent attire.

Come Friday! Yours affectionately, JOYCE.

DEAR BRAT—We've been waiting for Kenton's picture to send you, so there has been delay, but I hope you will get this in time for your landing.

I've had two offers of principalship—one in Hamilton, Bermuda, and one in Pompton Lakes, N. J. I probably will not go to Bermuda. I went to New York last night to see about the Pompton Lakes job, and I think I stand a good chance of getting it.

By now you know of my Memorial sonnet on George Meredith, which appeared in last Thursday's New York *Sun*. I enclose copy of it.

It is very hot here. Kenton is asleep. He looks pretty well now; he's not such a bad-looking child.

I have bought a new book by Kenneth Grahame, called "The Wind in the Willows." You remember, you liked his "Dream Days" and "The Golden Age" so much.

There is, of course, still a chance of my going to New Wilmington, Pennsylvania, to teach in the college there— Westminster College it is called.

We are going to move next Monday. Just address my letters Morristown, N. J., until June 25.

I will write more very soon, but the postman is coming now.

Yours affectionately, JOYCE.

DEAR BRAT—I received a young letter from you recently. I knew you would break your accustomed resolution of isolation on shipboard—in fact you do not possess to any remarkable extent the qualities of a recluse.

I have had one poem printed since my Meredith sonnet in the *Sun*—a quatrain in *Moods*, a copy of which I enclose.

Today I received word from Professor Glen Swigget, of the University of the South, that he had accepted my poem "Prayer to Bragi" and would print it in an early number of his magazine, *The Pathfinder*. This magazine (not to be confused with a weekly news magazine of the same name, published in Washington) is probably the best sustained literary monthly in America, if not in the world. It prints nothing but poetry and essays, and numbers among its contributors Ludwig Lewissohn, Edith Thomas, Clinton Scollard, Henry Van Dyke and others of equal genius. My "Prayer to Bragi" is founded on a Norse legend of the origin of poetry. I read it to you once, and will send you a copy of it when it appears. My sonnet in the *Sun* has been reprinted in Morristown, New Brunswick, Norfolk and Newark papers, and has now passed into "Plate Matter," that is, into the syndicated "patent insides" that are sent around to country newspapers in various parts of the United States.

I do not know what I will do next year. I hope to get literary work of some kind. I have been offered three principalships, two in New Jersey and one in Bermuda, but I want literary work, not school teaching.

Well, be a good infant and write! Letters are preferable to postcards.

Yours affectionately, JOYCE.

Metuchen, N. J., August 7, 1909

DEAR BRAT—Naturally, I was much pleased with your enthusiastic praise of my "Ballade of Butterflies." I like it myself, and I thought it would appeal to you.

I have not started work with Funk & Wagnalls yet, as the arrangements are still unfinished. I received a letter from *Town and Country* recently, saying that they were sending me a book to review, and that they expected to use my services more frequently during the coming year.

I enclose a circular advertising "The Younger Choir," a book which is to consist of the work of a number of young writers of verse, including myself. Edwin Markham, who is to edit the book, wrote "The Man with the Hoe," and is a distinguished man of letters. Of the contributors, Viereck, Oppenheim and Van Noppen are the best known. Viereck is assistant editor of *Current Literature*, and a poet of some distinction. His play, "The Vampire," attracted much attention in New York last season. It is said that he has the right to wear the German Imperial arms—with the bar sinister. Oppenheim has the entrée to most of the magazines of importance. So has Van Noppen, who is a Lowell Institute lecturer. My father has ordered two copies in your name.

I have a rather rare Dickens book for you. It is a Dictionary of the Thames, written by the novelist when he was a young journalist. Aline is delighted with the egg and toast rack. So am I. So is Kenton. She has a birthday present to give you when you get back. I have another present for you, too, but I won't tell you what it is. However, it's nice. I saw it in New York and thought you might like it.

We dined with Sflager last night. She sent her love to you. She is looking very well.

I am glad you are having a good time. I think you will enjoy next winter while we are in New York. We'll have large times! I am at work on a novel.

Yours affectionately, JOYCE.

HELLO BRAT!—Hope you enjoyed your birthday. Enclosed find fifteen (the correct number, I believe, with one over) enthusiastic embraces and an equal number of severe blows upon what may delicately be designated the back of your stomach. Kenton eagerly says the same.

I sent you a red leather portfolio. Use it to write me, imp and fiend that you are! Lord, I've written twenty letters to your one this summer!

We went to the Parkers' tea today—Aline in her reception gown, and I in my grey suit with my stick and new Panama hat.

You remember the poem "Rose and Grey" which was suggested to me by Mr. George Bailey's letter? It has been accepted by *The Bang*. This magazine is devoted almost exclusively to verse, and is edited by Alexander Harvey, who is editor also of *Current Literature*. It is a very high-class magazine, and entry to its pages is a thing greatly to be desired. I enclose Mr. Harvey's letter of acceptance.

Practically every one at the tea asked after you. Miss Molt said, "I don't ask if she's having a good time—she carries a good time wherever she goes!"

I am darn glad you are sailing sooner than you expected! So is Aline! So is Kenton! Kenton wishes an answer to his postcard. You will like my Panama hat. It cost five dollars. During this hot weather Kenton wears only a band and a pair of diapers. He has no teeth.

Well, be a good brat! Go to London by all means if you get a chance! And write me a letter for the love of Heaven!

Yours affectionately, JOYCE.

DEAR BRAT—This is the eighth letter written since hearing from you. Enclosed find a picture of Morristown High School faculty. I mentioned it before and meant to send it, but mislaid it. I am in the lower right-hand corner. Mr. Morey is seated just above me. The other man in the picture is Dr. Pierson. He is in the picture because of his position as president of the Board of Education. Miss Brown (the assistant principal) whom you met at Lakeside Place, is the lady in the centre of the top row. Miss Slack, whom you also met, is next to Dr. Pierson.

I have just this evening concluded some work I have been doing for *Red Cross Notes*. I am now at work on a special article for the *Literary Digest* on the French view of Meredith. I will send you a copy of the issue in which it appears. In it I make a translation from M. Charles Chasse's article "La France dans l'Oeuvre de Meredith" in *La Revue* for June 15. I will also send you the August *Moods* and the August *Pathfinder*, in both of which I have poems—"Tribute" and "Prayer to Bragi."

I bought your present in New York yesterday. It is large and red, and is coming not by post, but by mail. Try and deserve it by writing occasionally in the intervals of wall climbing and general raising of Heck.

Kenton and Aline send love. They are wailing and cursing for lack of letters from you. Kenton said last night, "Some English infant has cut me out."

Yours with love, JOYCE.

New Brunswick, N. J., 1909

DEAR BRAT—Received an amiable young letter from you today. Aline was delighted with her pendant. She has recently started to wear black ribbons around her throat and she likes the pendant to hang on it. By the way, the red portfolio was not from Aline and myself, as I have several times distinctly stated! It was from me! Aline is making a birthday present for you, which will be ready on your arrival.

My work with Funk & Wagnalls does not start until about Sept. 10, so temporarily I am working at the factory, making a fool book about window displays. God help the druggist who decks his window after my suggestions! Speaking of God, Arthur Devan called last night. He was much embarrassed when Kenton appeared in his nightgown to greet him. When he departed, Arthur shook hands with Aline and remarked, "Good night, Buster!" immediately turning purple and explaining that he meant Kenton, not Aline, by this laudatory title.

I expect to be down to meet you when you return, unless my Funk & Wagnalls work has begun then. Even if it has, I will see you that evening, for we're going to stay with you until October first. I'll commute from New Brunswick to New York.

Kenton is writing you a letter to go by this same mail.

Yours affectionately, JOYCE.

I'll be darn glad to get you back home!

171

DEAR BRAT—McAlister and I did not stay long with the Higher Education Association. The magazine was a visionary impalpable thing, not to come into being for some months. Meanwhile our work as assistant editors was to consist not in preparing copy nor writing anything, but in selling stock, an occupation for which we were not particularly fitted or inclined. Also, the stock was speculative in the extreme—so much so that a blind kitten of average discretion would refuse to invest therein. Accordingly, especially since we were to sell stock on commission, not on salary, we resigned. McAlister is now a night reporter on the *Sun;* I have got a job with Funk & Wagnalls, the publishers of the *Literary Digest.* My work will begin August 1st, and will consist chiefly of preparing articles on modern French literature and reading French books submitted to the house for publication. I do not know what the salary will be. If I don't like that job—or if Funk & Wagnalls don't like me—I have a chance to enter the book department of Scribner's on Sept. 1st. In either case we will live in New York, which ought to gratify you. We will take you to dinner at the Café Boulevard, where they have an amiable roof garden and a Hungarian orchestra in costume, and a man with a mandolin, who sings in Hungarian and Italian.

By the way, try and procure and learn two Italian songs, one of which goes "Chimiminimi!" and the other of which is called "Finiculi Finicula." The second is about a gravity railroad on Mt. Vesuvius.

Kenton insists on preventing me from sleeping in the morning, when left on the bed, by crawling after me and punching me. He does not cry much, but he converses and laughs loudly all the time. His eyes are brown. Helen Hardenburgh thinks he looks like you.

I enclose a copy of a Ballade I wrote recently, also a picture of some boys who were in the Morristown High School. While I have had several chances to teach school at a good salary, I had rather do literary work for smaller pay.

Be a good infant!   Yours affectionately, JOYCE.

147 College Ave., New Brunswick, N. J., 1909

Dear Brat—I received an amiable young letter from you recently, and I was darned glad to get it, for I'd been feeling rotten about not getting any while my father was getting a lot.

I start work in New York a week from Monday with Funk & Wagnalls. The tunnel under the river is done now, so I do not need to cross by the ferries. This saves a good deal of time. I expect to go to New York on business next week early. I hope you get your present in time for your birthday. Furthermore I hope you like it!

I saw the picture Ferguson drew of you. He may be a worthy youth, but nevertheless with all deference I beg to state that the picture is a damnable caricature and that I should enjoy making him eat it.

Kenton does not cry much but he laughs and shouts loudly, waving his arms. He delights to do this mornings when I wish to sleep. Furthermore he catches my hair and endeavors to rise by means thereof. He took an unlit cigar from me the other day and began to eat it. I stopped him, as it was a good cigar.

NOTICE—See the pageant at Bath if you get a chance! It's going to be especially good. Also, by all means go to London! You will be very foolish if you neglect to.

Aline and I dined with the Corbins last Wednesday. Sflager said she had a letter from you and intended to write soon. She is looking very well now. She sleeps out on a balcony.

Well, for Heaven's sake, write occasionally! Aline and Kenton send love! Both will write soon.

Yours affectionately, Joyce.

173

DEAR BRAT—Allow me to remark that this is the *fourth* letter I have written since hearing from you! My Yorkshire pipe is accumulating an excellent cake. I am spending most of my time nowadays reading French, as my work with Funk & Wagnalls will be largely in the line of reading French books and manuscripts.

Kenton is growing considerably human, and sends his love. He seems to be fond of Maria, whom he usually has with him. He is now out on the porch sleeping in his carriage, and secured from flies by means of mosquito netting.

If you happen to see Mr. Bailey this summer, remember me to him. I suppose we'll start in securing a flat in New York soon. My office will be 44 West 23rd St., right near the shopping district, so it will be easy for you to go out to lunch with me when you come to New York. We will go to Dorlon's, which is next door to my office, or to Cavanagh's, which is only two blocks off, or to the restaurant in the basement of the Flatiron Building, which is on the next corner. I have discovered an amiable drink, which I am eager to see you consume. It consists of equal parts of French Vermouth and Cassis, and is served in a cocktail glass.

It seems to me you might write to me at least as often as you do to my father! I've written to you certainly as often as he has, if not more often. If you didn't get the letters, Timpson didn't forward them, that's all, for I've written every week since you left except the week we were moving into the boarding house, and the following week I wrote twice. Yet my father gets letters every other day, while Kenton and I are left in the cold.

I expect to send your birthday present off the first part of this week. I hope you like it—it's a present worthy of an amiable, intelligent letter-writing infant—try to deserve it! I am going shares on my father's present to you, but this is a separate, distinct and individual additional present, such as no other infant, however worthy, ever received.

In the next issue of *Moods*, which appears August 1st, I have a poem. I have a poem also in the *Pathfinder* for August. By the way, I told you about the *Pathfinder* poem about a month ago, and you didn't mention it. Do you remember receiving the letter? *Moods* is a large and prosperous magazine now, as large as the *Strand*, and numbering among its contributors Julia Marlowe, George Sylvester Viereck, Percy MacKaye and myself.

Seaumas O'Shiel has become a Socialist.

Kenton wears white woolen socks as a cure for colic. Did you ever hear of that remedy? You might try it as a preventive of seasickness.

Well, we'd be having a darned sight better time if you were here. That's straight, and not intended as flattery, for in several respects you are an infant worthy of considerable enthusiastic approval.

Yours affectionately, JOYCE.

125 Wadsworth Ave., New York City, 1909

Mrs. Kilburn-Kilmer.

Dear Brat—Enclosed find a poem which you may perhaps like. Next Thursday I am to start translating a Russian play, "The Cherry Garden," with a friend of mine who is an exiled Revolutionist. He will put it into English and I will revise the English. It will then be published as a separate volume by Moods Publishing Co. Of course we won't make any money out of it, but it will be amusing.

I am working for Funk & Wagnalls now at $15.00 a week. The work is pleasant and the hours are short, and the associations are most desirable.

Come out soon! My lunch hour is from 12:30 to 1:30. My office is on 23rd Street, right by the Subway.

Yours affectionately, Joyce.

———

New York, Dec. 22, 1909

Dear Brat—Don't be an idiot! We decided yesterday evening, long before your infantile letter came, that we would come to New Brunswick Friday, Christmas Eve, in time for dinner, and stay over night and to dinner next day. One advantage of so doing is that Kenton can hang up his sock by the gas logs. He has teething rings made out of biscuit.

If you are a good child I'll give you the nicest Christmas present you ever got from me. If not you'll get spanked so that you will have to eat your Christmas dinner off the piano.

Yours affectionately, Joyce

My Good Infant—Help! Puff's birthday is the 21st, and according to your own statement and our agreement, it is to be celebrated not this coming Sunday, but Easter Sunday, the 27th! And Aline is to have her new hat finished by that date, and her new suit, and I am to wear my Prince Albert and perhaps if it's a fine day we will parade to church and distract the general attention from Comrade Elisha Brooks's sermon.

You said, "Shall we celebrate Puff's birthday the 21st or on Easter Sunday?" I said, "On Easter Sunday, because I may get Good Friday and Easter Eve off!" You said, "Good." Puff said, "Good indeed."

And get to the office before 12:30 Thursday. I have a new luncheon place—and I guarantee the production of King —absolutely! Will hand you your gift Thursday.

Say, there may possibly be rather important results from an interview I am to have with Charles Thompson, John A. Moroso and some other people this Saturday evening! But don't say anything about it until I tell you definitely. I may leave Funk & Wagnalls for much more desirable work. I'll tell you more about it Thursday.

So, you see, we may spend Good Friday, Easter Eve, and Easter Day in New Brunswick. Be a good child!

Yours affectionately, Joyce.

DEAR BRAT—There is a strike in Philadelphia, so come here by 12:30 Thursday, and we will lunch at the Fifth Avenue restaurant—on Fifth Avenue near 24th St.

"Jesus and the Summer Rain" was in Sunday's *Call*.

Saturday night we had the first meeting of our new magazine staff. Don't say anything about it, or I'll be fired from Funk & Wagnalls! I'll tell you all about it when I see you.

Find out what clothes of mine are in New Brunswick!

Puff says you told him he could eat fruit-cake and drink champagne at his party. He ate his postcard this morning with great satisfaction, before he was detected.

Yours affectionately, JOYCE.

New York, Oct. 21, 1910

DEAR BRAT—Here is the clipping concerning Simpson. We went up to the apartment last night. The Subway was blocked, so we took a surface car, which took about two hours.

That was a very delightful luncheon yesterday. I hope you enjoyed Glenzer and the show.

Yours affectionately, Joyce.

New York, Dec. 1, 1910

DEAR BRAT—Enclosed find the letter for Glenzer. It is a very nice letter. That card I showed was simply an invitation to an evening at the Authors' Club, not a membership card. I am not eligible to join until I publish a book.

Tell my father I am collecting the book catalogues he required. Come out! Yours affectionately, JOYCE.

DEAR BRAT—Enclosed find poem. The *Times* gave me only $6.00 for "Chevley Crossing," so I have quit giving them stuff. L——— is no longer editor of the Sunday *Times*, and the present occupant of his position probably never read any verse before he got his present job. I won't bother with the *Times* at all until the present Sunday editor is fired or mercifully killed.

Barry says he received a charming letter from you. He also reproved me for failing to inherit your laugh. Slip, slap, slop.

Let every one pray for the soul of Edward VII. He needs it.

We dined at the Petitpas the other night. There were old Mr. Yeats, Eric Bell, Snedden, Kraymborg, Hartpence, Van Wyck, Brooks, Aline and myself. Then we went to Henri's studio. Norman Poe and Ellen Terry's son and numerous other people were there.

Yours affectionately, JOYCE.

Jan. 3, 1910

DEAR BRAT—My "Butterfly Ballade" was in the magazine section of yesterday's New York *Times*. I had forgotten that I had sent it to them. They have in their possession also my "King's Ballade," which I suppose they will print soon.

Be a good child!

Yours affectionately, JOYCE.

DEAR BRAT—The question is, does the postcard you sent my father—I got none!—represent "Nymph and Swineherd" or "The Suffragette and the British Workman"? It is, at any rate, an interesting picture.

I had two bits of verse in today's *Times*—"Love's Rosary," which you have seen, as I wrote it last year in Morristown, and "Love's Thoroughfare," a recent sonnet. I am sending you (by my father, who steams Tuesday) the magazine section of the *Times* containing these verses and also a poem by Shaemas, and another by my friend John A. Moroso, of whom I spoke to you.

Puff has asked me to enclose one of his pictures for you. He has had rather a hard day, combining indigestion with rolling down the porch-steps. He is peacefully sleeping now and will be all right tomorrow.

Puff has a large vocabulary nowadays, and an ingratiating manner. He is not reading so much as formerly, however.

We are going to dinner with my father tomorrow night at Luchow's. Then we are going back to New Brunswick, and my father will stay over night at a hotel or on the boat. I have a number of new pieces of verse to show you when you return, and I am looking forward to our Thursday luncheons with much pleasure. Also you have a birthday present awaiting you.

Yours affectionately, JOYCE.

DEAR BRAT—We are going out to New Brunswick in the motor car Saturday afternoon.

Much obliged for insane but amiable group pictures. One male god-child of yours is fairly attractive. I don't know whether it's a Sharp, a Woolard or a Starling. You certainly are looking prosperous.

We are all recovered now from our various ailments. I suppose you are tremendously excited over the Jeffries-Johnson fight on July 4th. I will cable you the result collect.

This letter has been lost for several days. I have just found it and will complete it.

Johnson defeated Jeffries, as I suppose you have heard. My sonnet "Court Musicians" was in Sunday's *Times*. I'll send you a copy. We are all out in New Brunswick.

It is now about the ninth of July. Hereafter I will finish my letters at a sitting, as this business of writing at odd intervals seems to delay the completion of an epistle indefinitely.

By way of a mid-summer recreation, I decided to have my throat expurgated yesterday, so I had two physicians out to remove my tonsils.

Wait till you see your birthday present!

Thank you for the Thrushes. I anticipate their arrival with great pleasure.

By the way, while you are in England, by all means take in some of the seashore resorts like Brighton or Folkstone. That is a feature of English life, apparently distinctive and interesting.

Yours affectionately, JOYCE.

DEAR BRAT—We went to New York to move our furniture into our new apartment, and have just got back. We have an apartment with the same number of rooms as before, but very much larger, with electric light, and front instead of rear, and the rent amounts to only a quarter a month more. It's on 184th Street—about as far from the Subway as before. You have a large room with very fine golden paper! Take advantage of it! Furthermore, you have a present waiting for you—your birthday present, in fact!

Puff has been visiting his friend Mollie Campbell in Metuchen, and returned to New Brunswick today. He is eagerly anticipating your return, and intends to start shaving soon.

The pipe you sent me has two hats now. It smokes excellently, and I think the wood will grow darker. You certainly showed discretion in the selection of the stem and mouthpiece.

We called on Sflager last Sunday. She is looking well.

I wonder if you saw "The Blue Bird" in London. I think it must be much better worth seeing than "Chanticleer."

Your friend Roosevelt has been elected temporary chairman of the Republican party convention.

I hear that the ladies of London now smoke slender Japanese pipes instead of cigarettes.

I have written a number of poems that you will see on your return. I am going to send some to two London publications—the *Spectator* and the *New Age*, both of which are very interesting weeklies.

Well, we'll see you before long. We'll all try to get down to the dock to see you land, if we find out when the boat comes in, which we probably will be able to do.

Yours affectionately, JOYCE.

DEAR BRAT—We are on the shore of a very large lake. Our cottage is on the side of a mountain. The lake is surrounded by mountains which come right down to the water. Last night it snowed, and this morning there is snow on top of the mountains across the lake. We have a motor boat and several row-boats. We row and walk a good deal. It is very cold but we have a big open fire of birch logs.

The reviews in the New Brunswick papers were very good. You are an admirable press-agent. Much obliged!

The day before I left I was told that Mr. Pickering, the head of the illustration department of the Dictionary, was leaving because of ill health. Mr. Vizetelly offered me his job (Mr. Pickering's, not Mr. Vizetelly's) and I accepted it. I have an assistant. I don't know anything about illustrations, but I'll make my assistant do the work.

I'm glad Reed's is going to carry my book in stock. I told the Baker & Taylor Co. to write to him. I hope he sells some.

I suppose the convention is now convening. How exhilarating. Thank you for the watch and for sending Stewart Walker the pictures. I hope my father is by this time in good health.

In coming up here we left the boat at Albany. I remember visiting some cousins or something there some years ago with you. They had a translation of the "Divina Commedia" and a humourous connection by marriage. They lived up three flights of stairs. Who were they? They had a cat and several kittens.

Kenton is clamouring for exercise, so I guess I'll let him row us across the lake to post this letter.

Be a good infant. I certainly am obliged to you for those notices. I will be glad to see you again.

Aline and Kenton send love.

Yours affectionately, JOYCE.

Dear Brat—I will be very glad to have you with me Thursday at 12:30. Get to the office about 12:20 if you can. Furthermore, I'll pick out a nice matinée for you to go to.

Didn't a copy of the January *Pathfinder* come for me? If it did please bring it, and any other mail I may receive.

Remember that Thursday is the day you're coming—I have luncheon engagements for Tuesday and Wednesday.

You were particularly fashionably attired when last you appeared. I may introduce you to Mr. King, if he's around when you're on hand Thursday.

I finished the article my father wished, and am sending it to him by this mail.

By the way, Mrs. Trask's play,"The Little Town of Bethlehem," is at Madison Square Garden Theatre, not the New Theatre. It started a week ago today, that is, the 17th, and was scheduled to run only 16 performances. So if you're going to it, you'd better get busy.

Yours affectionately, Joyce.

Dear Brat—I have now completely recovered from the measles, and am back at work again. Now Kenton has the ailment, but we expect he will be well by the time you get this letter. I am sending a copy of *The Forum*, which contains Le Gallienne's review of "The Younger Choir," in which he pleasantly mentions my Ballade.

During my illness I asked Aline what time it was late one night. For answer she arose, fast asleep, and in the pitch darkness handed me the alarm clock and went back to bed.

If you happen to run across any of the publications of The Samaurai Press, of Surrey, will you send me a copy if they seem worth while? I think they cost a shilling each. And will you please notice what London papers and magazines print most verse, and send me their addresses?

I lunch at the Columbia Club nowadays, and the dining room is outdoors on a pavilion now. As it is right in Grammercy Park, it is very charming.

Do you hear much of Ezra Pound's work in England? He is a young American poet resident in London. I have read his two books, which have made some sensation over here.

Mitchell Kennerly has succeeded Russell Hertz as editor of *The Forum*. Barrie has gone to the country, rejoicing in what he called a delightful letter from you. Mr. King is in Paris now.

We are going to Lake George in August, to a cottage belonging to Mrs. Spencer Trask, for a couple of weeks.

Remember me to George the Five. Much obliged for the paper with account of Ed's funeral. I am using black ink on account of the court mourning.

Yours affectionately, Joyce.

DEAR BRAT—I will not apologise for using red ink, as I think it has a rather decorative effect. Numerous postcards have been received from you by Puff, Aline and myself, but no letter for the past eighteen years. You have not yet stated whether or not you approved the coronation. Give my love to Emily Grigsby, when you are next at court. That Grigsby affair is absolutely delightful. I have seen her often in New York, and several friends of mine know her well. She is a very beautiful and brilliant woman. She certainly has fooled the respectable people concerned.

Puff has been wandering about during the recent hot weather clad in his rompers, with no other garment. He climbs up and down stairs incessantly, and has developed a certain faculty for narrative.

My book is progressing, as is our song. One of your postcards to Aline said that you had made a tune for "Terre d'Amour." I am, strange to relate, interested in that fact, and, remarkably enough, would be glad to have the tune.

Shaemas has brought out his book, which is very good indeed. I think, however, that in form mine will surpass it. You will, of course, receive a special advance copy, before the others are made. How did you like "Madness"? The *Digest* reprinted it this week from *Harper's Weekly*, and although you have a copy of the poem already, I am sending a clipping to refresh your memory.

By the way, Aline told you we bought a lot to build a house on, didn't she? It's really more accessible than our apartment was. We are going to build a house with a large fireplace and built-in bookcases, and a bright red room for you!

Yours affectionately, JOYCE.

DEAR BRAT—I think I have told you eighteen times how much I liked the books you sent me, but nevertheless I now again inform you that they are delightful. Shane Leslie is one of the most brilliant of the younger Irish writers, and as he has no American publisher, his books are difficult to procure over here. The "Anthology of French Verse" is one I have never before seen, and is, I think, the best collection of the sort that I know. You certainly know how to buy books, my good infant.

By the way, how did you like the birthday poem I sent you? And I'm going to give you another birthday present when you come back, and so is Aline, and so is Puff. And you'll have a red room in our new house! I am reviewing books for the New York *Post*. They have printed two, and have sent me three more novels to review for the next issue. Aline is delighted with the prospect of receiving a sun-dial. We have wanted one very much. We shall probably put it on a post in the front yard, or fasten it to a great boulder that is already there.

Mr. Guy's poem got through the Customs House all right, and was received by us. Reverencing the Cloth as I do, I refuse to repeat Puff's comments on Mr. Guy as a poet. The mug, however, was admirable. He has two coronation mugs now, both china, one from you and one from Mr. Guy. He demands a third, which shall be of enamelled tin, unbreakable.

I miss our Thursday luncheons very much, and have found numerous delightful places where we will eat on your return. Also there is an opera coming to New York next winter, to which you are to be taken—Richard Strauss's "Rosenkavalier."

I am glad you saw the Coronation Procession, though I imagine you're fearfully sick of the affair by now.

Be a good infant and enjoy yourself.

Yours affectionately, JOYCE.

New Brunswick, N. J., 1911

DEAR BRAT—It's about time you wrote me a letter! I don't know yet whether or not you received your birthday poem. I am enclosing a clipping from *The Pathfinder*. I think you have seen the poem before. It refers to Arthur Symons, the great English poet, who is paralysed. He is only forty-five years old.

I read recently in a New Brunswick paper a brilliantly written letter from you. It is, I think, the most interesting piece of coronation literature I have read. You are certainly to be congratulated. I liked the simple and direct way in which you treated so elaborate and complicated a spectacle. It was a difficult thing to do, and you did it admirably.

Kenton and I took a walk over the Landing Bridge today. He has a large vocabulary, a fondness for narrative, vivid humour, and violent curiosity.

I was very glad recently to receive several books from you. "The Skipper's Wooing" is, I think, the best book of Jacob's that I have read. I had for a long time desired to read Dumas' "Black Tulip," and I found it charming. Conan Doyle is a comfortable old-fashioned sort of a writer, and I spent a very pleasant hour over the "Firm of Girdlestone." The Snaith book I have not yet read. Aline found it a most attractive romance, and so undoubtedly shall I.

I have been doing some reviewing recently for the *Nation*, a critical weekly, published in New York, somewhat resembling the English magazine of the same name.

Do you like King George as well as you did Edward VII? He is apparently a less interesting character.

Soon I will send you your specially bound advance copy of "Summer of Love." The small circular advertising it will be out soon, and mailed to the names on the list. I will also send you a number of the circulars to distribute from house to house and to paste on telegraph poles in London and York.

There is a possibility that in your room at Cragmere there will be a stationary wash-basin with hot and cold water! Would you like that? There are to be built-in bookcases, two open fireplaces, a dining porch and a sleeping porch. There is a spring on the grounds, and there are mountains all around. In fact, the house is to be built on a mountain side. Its name is to be Nine Bean Rows, after the poem by William Butler Yeats, called "The Lake Isle of Inisfree," which contains the lines:

> I will arise and go now, and go to Inisfree
> And a small cabin build there, of clay and wattles made.
> Nine bean-rows will I have there, and a hive for the honey-bee,
> And live alone in the bee-loved glade.

You are an excellent infant, and write very good letters, but you write them with annoying infrequency.

Enjoy yourself, my child, and bring back a large appetite and thirst for your Thursday luncheons.

Yours affectionately, JOYCE.

May 21, 1912

DEAR BRAT:—Hey, write a letter sometime! We expect to move Monday to Cragmere, Mahwah, New Jersey. The house isn't finished, but we think that one room will be ready for occupation by that time.

My father is sending you a copy of *The International*, containing "The Ballad of the Brave Wanton." I enclose copies of some poems which I think you have not seen.

My father, Aline and Kenton are in good health. So is Rosamonde.

I hope you are having a good time in England. When do you go to Ireland?

See as many pageants as possible. I've been reviewing the books of some American pageants recently for the *Times*. I will send you copies of the paper containing them.

Aline, Kenton and Rosamonde send love.

Yours affectionately, JOYCE.

DEAR BRAT—Thank you very much for the pipe! I have always wanted a carved meerschaum, and this is beautifully made. It is beginning to colour already. A part of the elephant's trunk is turning yellow. Eventually the whole pipe will be black, except the tusks, which, being made of ivory, will remain white. You could not have made a better selection.

Aline likes her plaques very much, and will write to you soon about them.

Last night we went to a dance at the home of some friends of ours. We can one-step and grape-vine. Aline grape-vines very well. When you come back I will teach you the new dances, unless you learn them while abroad.

The mountains about here are very interesting. Recently I climbed two of them with my friend Richardson Wright, who was visiting me. We found on Mt. Houvenkopf an old artist and his wife, the only white people for many miles. The natives live in log cabins and are called Jackson Whites. They are usually cream-coloured, but some of them are black and some are copper-coloured. They are of mixed Negro, Indian, German, Dutch and Scotch descent, their names being chiefly Dutch—Van Dick, De Grote and the like. They are very amusing people. There is a fine view from the mountains, and the valley between them is full of wild honeysuckle. You must climb these mountains this autumn.

Several postcards and an entertaining letter have come from you from Oxford—no one knew you were at Oxford. The postcards mentioned one "Arthur," your companion in much riot. We puzzled over Arthur for days. Finally your letter came and Arthur Devan was revealed.

Enjoy yourself, and occasionally receive a letter! I write about twice a week.

Yours affectionately, JOYCE.

June 25, 1912

DEAR BRAT—The sending of cables is a wearing occupation, and I think that the one I sent you yesterday is worth 10,000,000 letters.

Your two recent letters were very amusing, particularly the description of the picture of the automobile at the New Brunswick Boost Week Celebration.

We are living in Mahwah now. The floor and woodwork are not yet stained, and there is no electric light as yet, but otherwise we are very comfortable.

I am glad you liked "Martin" and "Pennies." The former did not allude to Martin Chuzzlewit or any other Dickens character; it was founded on an old man named Baldwin who used to work here.

I will be glad to have you market the poems in England, but this must be done after they have been printed over here. Otherwise the American rights are destroyed. I will tell you when to send them out.

Yours affectionately, JOYCE.

June 27, 1912

DEAR BRAT—Perhaps you would get my letters more surely and promptly if you gave me a complete itinerary, stating your whereabouts for this summer and autumn. Of course your letters state where you are, but you flit about considerably.

We are pretty comfortable in our house now. It is all finished except painting and staining. I went fishing Sunday and caught a large fat perch.

What do you think of Roosevelt now?

The poems mentioned cannot be sold to English magazines until they have appeared in American magazines. The fact that you sent "Pennies" to *The Spectator* is all right, but don't send any more out until I notify you that they have appeared over here. One of them, "A Blackbird and his Mate," will probably be ready in a few weeks, and I'll send you a copy to send out.

Send me an *Eye Witness*, please. Send Kenton a *Dublin Review*, please. Send Aline a box of tobacco, please. Send Rosamonde a stick, please, as she hopes to learn to walk.

Yours affectionately, JOYCE.

Cragmere, Mahwah, New Jersey, July 3, 1912

DEAR BRAT—Perhaps if you send me an itinerary, and I send letters to you direct, you will get them more surely.

Tomorrow is Fourth of July. Mac and James Gray and I are going fishing to Round Lake, about twelve miles from here. We will take a train.

I enclose some verses. I will send you soon two copies of *The International*, one containing a poem of mine, "The Ballad of the Brave Wanton," and the other containing a letter of mine in answer to Leonard Abbott's "Renaissance of Paganism."

When you get a chance please send me some copies of *The Eye Witness*, *The Dublin Review*, *The Spectator*, *The Academy*, *The Church Times* and *The Atheneum*.

Puff got stung on the mouth by a bee, but is otherwise in good health. He sends his love, and wants wooden shoes and a pipe. Aline and Rosamonde also send love. They want wooden shoes and a pipe.

Yours affectionately, JOYCE.

DEAR BRAT—I received a very amusing letter from you recently, and a copy of *The Spectator*. Thank you. I hope to receive more copies of *The Spectator*, also of *The Eye Witness*, *The New Age*, *The Dublin Review*, *The Academy*, *The Atheneum* and *The Church Times*.

I sent you today two copies of *The International*, one of them containing "The Ballad of the Brave Wanton," I think you received before, but I thought you might like to have this copy because it contains an article by Leonard Abbott on "The Renaissance of Paganism," which is answered by me in the July issue in an article entitled "The Renaissance of Your Grandmother."

Last week I had my tonsils and adenoids removed. I took ether, so it was not painful. I went to a very nice private hospital near Columbus Circle.

The postcard of the Wheat Sheaf Inn landlord (I think it was the Wheatsheaf Inn) and the figure from the ship are very amusing.

By all means read Chesterton's latest novel, "Manalive." I am reviewing it. It is a very delightful book. You remember those essays of Chesterton that I got you recently, don't you?

Before long it will be your birthday. Behave yourself, and you may get a nice present.

Yours affectionately, JOYCE.

July 23, 1912

Dear Brat—The music has arrived. I think the printers did excellent work. I am very proud to have my verses appear with such charming music.

You are supposed to be getting some birthday verses, but they will probably not arrive until after your birthday. I am going to share in the birthday present you get in England, and then when you land you will get three new birthday presents, one from me, one from Aline, and one from Kenton. Rosamonde is saving her money to meet the expense of being born.

Gray says by all means to go to Amplforth Abbey, which is a monastery near Coxwold. Several of the monks there are friends of his, particularly B. Parker. Gray is one of the editors here, whom you met. He is a Yorkshireman.

I hope you enjoyed the Scarborough pageant. The postcards show that you stopped in an attractive appearing hotel. By all means drink sherry-cobblers with mint crushed in them in hot weather, and mulled port in cold weather.

I thank you for a large number of *Spectators* and one *Eye Witness* recently received. Don't you find the *Eye Witness* a delightful weekly? Read Chesterton's "Manalive"; it's very good. I hope you enjoy your birthday. Many happy returns of the day! You'll get some birthday verses soon.

Aline, Kenton and Rosamonde send love.

Affectionately, Joyce.

Aug. 9, 1912

DEAR BRAT—Thank you for numerous excellent gifts—the pipe, which is a very fine briar, of the sort in which I especially delight, the "Pepy's Diary," which I have wanted to read for a long time, and the *Eye Witnesses, Spectators,* and a *Dublin Review.* I hope you got your birthday verses and that you liked them. Your birthday present you will receive on your return. Rosamonde wishes her poem at once!

Kenton has been somewhat ill, but has recovered. He wants a book. I enclose some verses which may interest you. My father is going abroad about August 20th, and has invited us to stay in New Brunswick during his absence. I do not know whether I can or not. I don't want to leave my house unoccupied.

The book of the Scarborough pageant was very interesting. Scarborough must be an amusing place. Did you go in swimming?

Why do you call the *Eye Witness* radical? It opposes the Insurance Act, and curses Lloyd George.

I am sending you a copy of the *Heptalogia* for the priest who wanted it, if you can remember which he was. It is the last copy on sale, as this edition is out of print. Give it to him, with my compliments, and tell him that American publishers and booksellers never take money from the clergy. I recommend you to read it, particularly "Disgust" and "The Person of the House." They are not at all proper reading for the British clergy! What have you been teaching the unsuspecting old person? Tell him to send me a copy of the *Oxford and Cambridge Review* and *The Church Times,* otherwise known as the *Sunday Punch.* By the way, the summer number of *Punch* which you sent me was very good.

Yours affectionately, JOYCE.

Cragmere, Mahwah, N. J., 1912

DEAR BRAT—I hope this letter reaches you—you are wandering about Germany, I suppose, and I feel a provincial distrust in the postal authorities of the Continent of Europe. I am writing regularly for the Book Review Section of the *Times* now, a long article every week. A week from tomorrow I leave my present job to become one of the editors of *The Churchman*. This may strike you as somewhat humourous. It is, perhaps, not without its amusing aspects.

I thank you for the various weeklies, which arrive regularly. I enjoy particularly *The Eye Witness*, which is, I think, a very brilliant publication. I told you how much I appreciated "Pepy's Diary." I received a copy of "Gifts of Shee," and was much pleased with its appearance. I certainly have cause to be grateful for your musical gifts. Thank my father, to whom I will write soon, for the two papers he sent me. Your latest letter (like most of them) was very amusing. The description of the bored youth with the wrist-watch was particularly entertaining.

I will write you a longer letter soon, but it's well into Monday morning now, and I must get up at six.

With love from Aline, Kenton and Rosamonde, and to my father, I am,

Affectionately yours, JOYCE.

Sept. 21, 1912

DEAR BRAT—Monday I start work on *The Churchman*, at 434 Lafayette St. The present manager of that paper was an instructor in English at Columbia when I was a student there, and he was manager of the Baker & Taylor Co. when they published my book. I am keeping up my articles in the *Times* and *The Digest*, and probably my Current Literature work.

I am looking forward eagerly to the renewal of our Thursday luncheons. My new office is not far from the St. Denis, so perhaps we shall make that the place for our meetings. It is a very good restaurant, as you probably remember.

Aline is much pleased with the jewelry you sent her, and will write to thank you soon. She will forward to Mrs. Alden and Constance the gifts you bought for them. They will be very glad to get them.

I am enjoying the magazines which you are sending, and I am looking forward to seeing you soon. Rosamonde, Aline and Kenton send love, as I do, to you and to my father.

Yours affectionately, JOYCE.

January 23, 1913

DEAR BRAT—I enclose card for the first of the Authors' Club receptions. It takes place, you see, on the afternoon of the day of the Dickens Fellowship Dinner.

The Poetry Society Dinner is next Wednesday. Tell me what colour gown you are wearing, so I can order especially good flowers.

Be a good child and I'll buy you some wax vestas.

My story in this Sunday's paper is about a typewriter-telegraph. I have a poem on the same page.

Yours affectionately, JOYCE.

199

Mahwah, N. J., May 4, 1913

Dear Brat—Thanks for the letters received recently,
written on the boat.

We went to a dance last night, and expect to go to another
next Saturday. Rose is gaining steadily and becoming very
good looking. There was a suffrage parade yesterday in New
York, but we didn't let her go to it.

I enclose some verses which you have not seen. "Servant
Girl and Grocer's Boy" is to appear in the *Smart Set*, and
"Trees" will probably appear in a magazine called *Poetry*.

It is very nice out here in the spring—there are large
numbers of violets, ranging in color from deep blue almost to
red, and some of them are striped light blue and white, also
there is an admirable dog-wood tree near the house, and we
have planted several vines.

Later I am going to send you some manuscripts and ask
you to try to sell them for me.

How are you getting along with the music you were to
have published? I am looking forward to receiving copies.

Yours affectionately, Joyce.

DEAR BRAT—As I write I smoke some of the admirable tobacco you sent me. The pouch is very nice. The meerschaum pipe has turned a beautiful brown and will soon be black—all except the tusks, which, being of ivory, do not colour.

The small photograph of you that accompanied the tobacco is amusing. The pictures with your godchildren were certainly excellent.

We are putting down a sand walk in front of our house, and we hope to put grass seed in soon.

I will send you copies of the *Smart Set*, the *Catholic World* and *The Bellman* containing some new verse of mine. Do you think you'll get a birthday present? Rose says you will, but she hasn't any sense. I was interested in the clipping you sent me in which my article was quoted from the *Times* Book Review, and I am enjoying the English magazines very much.

Yours affectionately, JOYCE.

DEAR BRAT—It's time I heard from you! Next week I am to lecture on Nicholas Nickleby before the Dickens Fellowship. Isn't that absurd? I may be president of it next year.

You said that you had forgotten the "Suicide" poem I sold to the *Smart Set*, so I send you herewith a manuscript copy. Kindly read it to eight vicars, two bishops and a cardinal. It will do them good, for it is a highly orthodox poem. I will send you a copy of the *Smart Set* for June containing it, and also a copy of the May *Catholic World* containing "Stars."

By all means see "The Hour and the Woman" at the Cosmopolis Theatre, Holborn, if it is given while you are in London. I suppose my father supplies you with copies of the *Times* Book Review, and it is probable that you can live without reading *The Churchman*.

Tell your clerical court that America is widely excited over the proposal to change the church name from "Protestant Episcopal" to "American Catholic." This question is to be decided at the Convention this summer, but undoubtedly the old name will be retained. The Convention is to be held in New York this year, you know, and I will probably attend some of the sessions.

I hope you had a pleasant trip and that you made the acquaintance of the Pages. I was not sure of their identity until I was on the dock. I think you met her at one of the Authors' Club teas during the past winter.

Eat plenty of large strawberries with thick cream and drink Whitbread's ale.

Yours affectionately, JOYCE.

Mahwah, N. J., 1913

Dear Brat—It was very pleasant to receive the magazines, which have come in accordance with my request. I was particularly glad to receive the copies of *The British Review*, which is a magazine I admire very much. *The Suffragette* came also, with the pin still fastened upon it.

I hope you enjoy your visit to London. You were wise to go there, I think. It seems absurd to visit England and spend no time in London.

I have a new job. I am working for the magazine section (not the book review) of the New York *Times*. For some months, you know, I have been dependent on book reviews and verse for a living.

Aline and I are delighted with the beautiful buckle you sent her. She is writing to thank you and to describe the Board of Health dinner in New Brunswick, which would have entertained you very much.

I sent you a copy of *The Catholic World* containing "Stars" and a copy of *The Churchman* containing a "Memorial Day" poem. If you have not received them, tell me and I'll send you other copies.

Yours affectionately, Joyce.

DEAR BRAT—I suppose by this time my father is with you. I am sending you two copies of the *Times* Book Review containing some special articles which I wrote. I will be glad when the dictionary work is over, so that I can devote more time to the pleasanter and more profitable occupation of writing.

Did you receive the *Heptalogia?*

The house looks pretty well now. I dug a blind drain to keep surface water from running into the cellar.

I am enjoying "Pepy's Diary." I had always wanted to read it. I have said this in two previous letters, but your letter recently received asks me if I got the book.

I hope you enjoyed Fr. Parker's call. Gray doesn't know him, but he knew his brother. Rosamonde enjoyed her poem, and should write and say so. As for the Yorkshire *Herald*, probably your conscience has by this time punished you sufficiently. It's all right, absurd infant!

Yours affectionately, JOYCE.

DEAR BRAT—Heaven knows where you are now—presumably in Italy.

Be sure to let me know by what boat you are sailing, at what time and from what port! If in Italy you happen to see a good wall crucifix of iron, brass or bronze—not of wood—I'd like very much to have it.

I have in this Sunday's *Times* Book Review a poem in memory of Mme. Faure, who died last month. She wrote over the name of "Pierre de Coulevain." I think you read her novel, "Sur La Branche" ("On the Branch"). She was an old maid who travelled alone all over Europe, living in hotels and writing novels about the people she saw. The title "On the Branch" refers to her mode of life, her flitting from hotel to hotel. I am sending you a copy of the paper containing the poem, but since papers are delivered less surely than letters, I am sending also a manuscript copy.

I expect to bring out another volume of verse this November. The book is to be dedicated to—to whom do you suppose? Why, to you if you are a good child! Think of that!

Did you see my poem called "To Certain Poets" in the October *Smart Set?* The *Smart Set* is published in England as well as America, I believe. I sent you a copy of *The Bellman*, containing "St. Alexis," but I have not seen mention of it in your letters.

The *Home News* ran your letter with these head-lines: "Mrs. F. B. Kilmer Has Success with Her New Songs. Nearly all the Edition of 'Before the Fair' Sold—Likes London—Asks Policeman Where to Get Hairpins. Is the Guest of Noted People."

It is a very good letter. I have cut it out and saved it for you. Well, enjoy yourself.

Yours affectionately, JOYCE.

Dear Brat—I hope this reaches you when you land. I have just finished writing a review of Alfred Noyes' "Tales of the Mermaid Tavern." It is an admirable book; you must read it. Aline has sold two poems to *Harper's Weekly*, and I have sold "Stars" to *The Catholic World*. I'll send you a copy when it is printed, which will be during the present month. I hope you enjoyed your trip and made the acquaintance of the Pages, for I am now sure it was they. We did not recognise them, however, until we left the boat.

My father is coming out for a week-end soon. I hope that by the time you get back you will find vines growing about our house. We are going to plant some soon.

I am getting a higher rate of pay from the *Times* now, which helps considerably.

Be a good brat, and buy yourself two reception gowns.

Yours affectionately, Joyce.

April 20, 1914

DEAR BRAT—Today the elevator starter (you always call him the "porter") in the Times Building said to me, "you ought to get a cable from your mother soon." And tonight my father telephoned that you had landed.

Now I should say "not a word from you yet!" and lament that you didn't send me a letter by the pilot. I hope you had a comfortable trip.

There is soon to be, it seems, a war with Mexico. Probably it will be declared tonight. Mr. Ihlseng—you remember his wife, who is very active in the Dickens Fellowship—is in Mexico, and Mrs. Ihlseng is very much worried about him. The war will be over in a month or so, but there will be fighting with the bandits in the hills for years, just as there is still in the Philippine Islands.

You have bought, I suppose, the May *Smart Set* with my poem "Delicatessen." I will send you the May *Smart Styles*, which contains my essay on alarm-clocks—it is called "The Wiban Chanticleer."

Eat English mustard on roast beef, and lemon juice on chops. Drink a mixture of white crème de menthe and brandy before meals, since English cocktails are bad.

Yours affectionately, JOYCE.

April 30, 1914

DEAR BRAT—Finally I got a letter from you; this morning, in fact. I'm sorry you had a dull voyage, but I know you'll make up for it rapidly. I hope you enjoy the Dickens Pageant, or whatever it is that you are attending as representative of the Dickens Fellowship of New York.

'I will send you a copy of *Smart Styles* containing my essay on alarm-clocks. I suppose you have read the *Smart Set* with my poem' "Delicatessen."

In London there is a paper called *The Standard*. In a recent issue it contained an article about my translation of the new-found stanzas of "The Rubaiyat," which appeared in the copy of the *Times* that I gave you when you sailed. But the author of the article called me Miss Joyce Kilmer, and spoke of the Evening *Times*.

The Dickens Fellowship gives an entertainment at the Waldorf Saturday. Tom Ferris, an English actor, is to do Dickens impersonations. Next year we'll give a play every month, and you will be Mrs. Nickleby and anything else you like!

Yours affectionately, JOYCE.

May 27, 1914

Dear Brat—I got a very nice letter from you today. I am glad you are enjoying the Dickens Fellowship business. The picture illustrating my poem "Trees" is not the drawing which appeared in a magazine called *Scouting*, which reprinted the poem, but a photograph mounted on a grey cardboard panel, with the poem lettered underneath.

I have written a one-act play called "Some Mischief Still." It is a satire on Feminism, and will appear in the *Smart Set*. It may be produced in vaudeville, if I have good luck.

Sir Arthur Conan Doyle is now in New York for a brief stay. I expect to interview him soon.

Did Montagu come to see you yet? I gave him your address, and he said he wanted to call on you.

Don't eat vegetable marrow; it's a foolish vegetable. Eat English mustard on roast beef. In hot weather, take a tall glass, put in two fingers of Gordon gin, one finger of lime juice, plenty of cracked ice and fill with lemon-soda. Let it get very cold and you will find it an excellent drink. And don't put sugar and water in your claret, unless it's very bad. White mint and brandy shaken up together with cracked ice make a good substitute for a cocktail.

Yours affectionately, Joyce.

May 30, 1914

Dear Brat—I don't owe you a letter, but nevertheless I write. I have received several copies of London newspapers from you, which were very interesting. Much obliged.

We are making quite a garden out at Mahwah, or rather, Aline is. I am too busy to be able to do much about it.

What was the name of the Canadian Pacific Railway Company's boat we sailed on once? Of course, you have read of the Canadian Pacific boat that sank in the St. Lawrence.

Conan Doyle is over here now. I did not interview him for the *Times*, because I was busy interviewing Justin Huntley McCarthy (who wrote "If I Were King") and a Hungarian named Dr. Farkashozy.

Kenton enjoys his map of England tremendously, and can put it together as well as I can, or better. He is planning an early visit to the Circus.

Yours affectionately, Joyce.

June 6, 1914

DEAR BRAT—I hope you enjoyed the Dickens Convention. We will probably have a show next year, something like the trial of, whatever his name was, for the murder of Edwin Drood, that they had in London and in Philadelphia last year, only we'll have Dickens himself as defendant, try him for being a back-number or a sentimentalist or something of the sort. What do you think of the idea? By the way, if you can get a full account of the trial that the London Dickens Fellowship had, I'll be much obliged.

My version of the new quatrains of Omar Khayyam, which was in the copy of the *Times* I gave you when you sailed, is being used in some way in connection with the play "Omar the Tentmaker," now running in San Francisco. If it comes back to New York in the autumn, we'll go to see it—perhaps we'll have a box given us.

I suppose by now you have received Aline's letter saying how much she liked her excellent sash. It is certainly a beautiful thing. I am smoking my pipe and find it very good indeed. Also young Kenton enjoys his map.

Yours affectionately, JOYCE.

June 11, 1914

DEAR BRAT—This morning I received the book "Dickens Land" and two copies of the Rochester Dickens Fellowship magazine. Thank you. I am glad to see that you sang, especially that you sang "The Yellow Gown," which is, I think, your best song. But they are all good.

Rose is in good health, having recovered from a slight poison-ivy.

What do you think you'll get for a birthday present?

I enclose a sonnet that I have not yet sold. Houvenkopf is a mountain. Yours affectionately, JOYCE.

211

DEAR BRAT—I suppose you are enjoying Yorkshire now. Thank you for the Yorkshire papers recently received.

We were, of course, much exercised about the robbery, and glad that you recovered your property. Your story of the affair was most graphic and entertaining; I enjoyed it tremendously, but I confess that I am somewhat bewildered. This, at least, is clear—a villainous Spanish girl had designs on a virtuous chief of police, and you rescued him by sitting up in bed and singing "Terre d'Amour," in a red kimono and boudoir cap. Then Scotland Yard was notified and Dr. Watson came with Sherlock Holmes and said that they would take care of your trunk. So you all went off to a Sunday-school treat, singing "The Yellow Gown."

Has Montagu been to see you yet? I don't know what his address is.

I will send you a copy of the July *Current Opinion*. I succeeded Leonard Abbot as editor of the Letters and Art Department, you know.

Don't forget that you are to suggest a title for my new book! It will appear early in September.

Yours affectionately, JOYCE.

July 1, 1914

DEAR BRAT—I hope you are enjoying Yorkshire. Your friends, the Suffragettes, seem to be spending a busy summer. It wouldn't surprise me for the American Suffragettes to adopt militant tactics soon.

Your account of the Liberal meeting was most amusing. Who told you you could heckle public speakers? The to'acco has not yet arrived, but I suppose it will be here by the time you get this letter. Thanks very much.

Rose seems to be gaining strength and is in excellent health. She has quite recovered from attack of poison-ivy. She seems to be steadily gaining strength in her arms and can now lift one hand to her mouth and feed herself, when she is lying down.

In Sunday's *Times* I have an article about a newly found poem of "Sappho," the discovery of which you may have seen noted in the London papers. I have made a translation of it into English "Sapphies," that is, into the same form of English verse. I will send you a copy, though I suppose my father keeps you supplied with American newspapers.

When do you go to Yorkshire? I suppose my letters will be forwarded if they arrive at The Norfolk after you leave.

Yours affectionately, JOYCE.

213

July 10, 1914

DEAR BRAT—Thanks for the excellent tobacco. It is very good indeed. I smoke it in that briar pipe you sent me; one of the best pipes you have given me. Kenton insists on swiping the "Dam family" pipe to blow soap-bubbles through.

I edited a symposium which appeared in last Sunday's *Times*, on "What Is the Best Poem in the English Language?" Twenty-five prominent English and American poets took part.

The publishers called the book "Trees and Other Poems." I think that the titles you suggested are much better, particularly "The Fourth Shepherd and Other Poems." But possibly that would make the book seem too devotional. "Trees" is my best-known poem, I believe. The book is dedicated to you, and so also is one of the poems, "Folly." I put "To A. K. K." as "Folly's" dedication, because I didn't want to repeat the dedication of the book.

I've got to go down to the publishers—be a good brat and take rum on grape fruit.

Yours affectionately, JOYCE.

———————

1914

DEAR BRAT—That is an excellent music box you sent Rose. She enjoys it very much and so do we. I remember that I had one like it, only round.

I am glad you are enjoying the Rochester Convention. The Dickens Fellowship meets tonight, and I will read a part of the report you sent me. I am glad to have the copy of the "Valentine" song. I have not had a chance to have it played yet, but I remember the excellent tune, and I want to hear you sing it.

I wrote a one-act play Sunday. It may appear in the *Smart Set.* I sent it to them first.

Enjoy yourself, and drink Barley Wine every day.

Yours affectionately, JOYCE.

DEAR BRAT—I think that that pipe you sent me is the best one you ever bought for me. It's not the most elaborate, of course, but it's an excellent pipe, good briar with a good bit, and it takes up very little room in my pocket. Thanks, very much!

I am glad you are enjoying London. Your account of the meetings of the Dickens Fellowship was most entertaining. You will probably have a very good time at Rochester.

I will get the elevator starter's (not porter's) last name and send it to you soon.

This afternoon I am going to Greystone, Mrs. Samuel Untermeyer's residence on the Hudson, in a special car with other members of the Poetry Society. Some of us are to read aloud on the lawn; it's a sort of a May festival. I will read "Trees" and perhaps "Old Poets."

Yours affectionately, JOYCE.

DEAR BRAT—You will receive a very nice birthday present indeed, if you are a good infant. Your birthday poem may not reach you on your birthday, because it's to be an extra special birthday poem, to be used as the dedication to "Trees and Other Poems." But you'll get it soon.

Did you see my poem "Waverly" in the London *Spectator*? I got a sovereign for it. It was reprinted in the London *Public Opinion*, which reprinted in the same issue my poem "The Bartender," from the *Smart Set*. This year is the one-hundredth anniversary of the publication of Sir Walter Scott's "Waverly," the first of the series which was called the Waverly novels.

I suppose you have seen my play, "Some Mischief Still," in the *Smart Set* by now. I hope you found it amusing. It may be brought out in book form by Vaughan and Gomme this autumn.

Your account of the lunatic in the train is most entertaining. I enjoyed it tremendously.

Be a good infant, and you'll get a good birthday present. And we'll have fun next winter.

Yours affectionately, JOYCE.

DEAR BRAT—I had a queer experience recently. I received a big square of grey cardboard on which some one had carefully lettered my poem "Trees" and pasted above it a beautiful photograph of a tree. I found out later that it had been done by a man out in St. Louis, Missouri, whom I do not know, and William Marion Reedy, editor of the St. Louis *Mirror* saw it and got him to send it to me. You can have it if you wish; it makes rather a nice decoration. I'll keep it till you get back, though; you won't want to carry it all over England.

Has Montagu been to see you yet?

I may give two lectures a week on English poetry at the Comstock School next year. I am going to see about it today. Are you going to Stratford-on-Avon? There is some special celebration there this year—or perhaps they had it last month. Enjoy yourself, and drink musty ale.

Yours affectionately, JOYCE.

April 29, 1915

DEAR BRAT—Here is a letter which I received after you sailed. I will have my Underwood & Underwood pictures developed and send one over to you. The pictures of you certainly are delightful.

I hope you get acquainted with George Arliss, if that was he whom we saw just before the boat sailed. He is a very great actor.

This is not a regular letter; it's just to carry the letter I am forwarding. I'll write you a regular letter soon. Be a good brat and enjoy yourself.

Yours affectionately, JOYCE.

1915

DEAR BRAT—Here is a picture taken Easter day. I don't think you have seen it before. It does not look particularly Eastery.

I enjoyed your two graphic letters very much. This certainly is an exciting time to be in England. Your letter about the soldier and his little boy was particularly interesting.

I told you, I think, about my visit to Hunter College, where I read several poems and saw Miss Cone, Miss Widemer and Miss Klauser. They all spoke affectionately of you—they had asked me to have you take dinner with them— and marvelled at your courage in sailing. Miss Cone said, when I said you had been asked if you were going to be a trained nurse, "The Uniform would be becoming to her!"

I read some poems at the First Congregational Church in Flushing one evening last week.

I hope you liked my "White Ships and the Red." I have received many letters about it. I received two today, although the poem was printed nine days ago. It was widely quoted.

I am much obliged for the numerous papers. The accounts of the anti-German riots were interesting. Did you see any of it?

I am sending a copy of a sonnet I wrote in memory of Lieutenant Rupert Brooke. He was a fine poet, who enlisted early in the war and died of sunstroke in the Dardanelles. I think he was the most gifted of all the younger English poets. The sonnet will probably appear in the New York *Nation* and I am also sending a copy to the London *New Witness*.

Be a good infant and enjoy yourself. Kenton, Rose, Deborah and Aline send love.

Affectionately yours, JOYCE.

1915

DEAR BRAT—Miss Widemer recently sent me the pictures which I enclose. She asked for your address, and said she'd send you a copy. She sent me also an absolutely delightful snapshot of you, which I am keeping, since she will send you another. I have given her your address.

I am enjoying *Punch* tremendously. All the other publications for which I asked you are coming regularly except *The New Witness*.

I enclose a circular announcing my lectures, although I have a vague recollection of having sent you one before. I expect to go out West lecturing in the late autumn and winter.

It looks now as if we'd get into war with Germany, but of course there is no way of knowing what will happen. At any rate, the war has awakened the United States to a sense of the necessity of adequate armaments. It is probable that we will have henceforth a large standing army and perhaps also a system of compulsory national service. It certainly would be a good thing.

The first Thursday after your return I will take you to Farrish's Chop House for luncheon, unless you want some place peculiarly American for a change. Farrish's is the only place in New York that I have found where they keep Burton ale—an admirable beverage which I hope you enjoy daily.

Be a good infant, and scare off Zeppelins with your umbrella.

Yours affectionately, JOYCE.

DEAR BRAT—I got the admirable pipe this morning. Thank you very much; it's just the sort of pipe I like. It has a persh stem, which is the proper sort of stem, and the bowl is made out of an excellent piece of briar.

Last week I went up to D'youville College, in Buffalo, to deliver a graduation address. D'youville is a very fine college for young ladies, conducted by the Grey Nuns. I am going there again to lecture on Lionel Johnson.

Naturally, the reports of bombs being dropped on England are disconcerting, especially since the papers do not give the names of the places struck. You certainly have selected a lively place for a holiday.

I am enclosing with this a few circulars of my book. I'll send more if you want them. I send also a copy of a poem which has not yet appeared in print.

Kenton is grateful for his postcards, and sends his love, as do the rest of the menagerie. As Kenton is learning to read print, he would appreciate receiving a postcard on which you had inscribed, in large letters, some brief and appropriate message which he could decipher for himself, such as, for example, THE BABY BITES THE CAT.

Be a good child and don't let England go prohibition.

Yours affectionately, JOYCE.

1915

DEAR BRAT—I don't think you can be getting all my letters. I notice you have not said anything about a little snap-shot of myself I sent you some weeks ago. Perhaps the censor got it. I'll send you one of the large pictures made by Underwood & Underwood some time this week. Also I will send you a copy of *Harper's Weekly*, containing an essay of mine called "Daily Travelling."

I am glad you liked the poem on Rupert Brooke. Did you receive one called "The Circus"?

I am glad to receive the papers you send me from time to time. You must take in all the shows and generally have as good a time as you can, because it does not do to be idle in a country situated as England is today; the atmosphere will distress you unless you amuse yourself.

Don't bother about the Dickens Fellowship. The New York Chapter will be tempted to secede unless it receives some recognition. It paid its dues to London for a long time, but got no benefit therefrom. Next year I'll have New York Chapter nominate you for vice-president of the main body.

Yours affectionately, JOYCE.

221

Dear Brat—You certainly should have received the Truth prize for the best *Lusitania* acrostic. Your poem was admirable; certainly the best of those printed. I showed it to my friend, Albert Crockett, who agreed with me that it was very good indeed.

I am enjoying the magazines and newspapers which you send me. Much obliged. The pipe is excellent, as I have already told you.

I am surprised that you failed to receive the little snapshot which I sent you. I enclose in this envelope a clipping from the *Book News Monthly*, in which the picture is reproduced. I will send you this week one of the Underwood & Underwood photographs.

We had not heard of the Zeppelin attack on Hull. Take care of yourself, adventurous infant, and stay inland. Buxton should be safe, I suppose. Fortunately, the Zeppelin attacks on England seem to be mainly spectacular.

What do you suppose you are going to get for your birthday present?

Yours affectionately, Joyce.

ACROSTIC ON THE *LUSITANIA*
(Referred to in Joyce's letter)

Let us remember to our latest day,
Under whose flag the devilish deed was done!
So let our children's children scorn the Hun!

In Hell's vast concourse every fiend was gay,
To know the thousands hurled beneath the wave,
At sunrise living—night an ocean grave.

Never shall Germany forgiven be!
In every heart where love and pity flame,
A murderer and the Kaiser are the same.

1915

DEAR BRAT—This evening's papers say that numerous Americans in London have been warned to leave the city. Were you warned? I don't suppose you'd leave, however, until you were good and ready to, if the Kaiser himself blew up Horrex's hotel. However, I imagine you'll find Coxwold more comfortable.

I can't remember whether or not I sent you a copy of my poem "Under Canvas." I enclose a copy anyway. I've sold it to *Lippincott's Magazine*.

I have enjoyed the papers very much, especially those with the accounts of the anti-German riots. I also was very glad to see the picture of Horrex's. We certainly had a good time in London last summer.

Rose is gaining in strength, under Miss Berg's ministrations. Deborah already can crawl around the bed, which is considered advanced for her age.

Try Gruyere cheese on soft toasted biscuit, with bottled port. An excellent combination, especially since you are where those commodities grow.

Yours affectionately, JOYCE.

DEAR BRAT—This evening I was looking through an anthology, and I came across "A life on the ocean wave, A home on the rolling deep." And who should be its author but your old friend Epes Sargent! Furthermore I find that he was born at Gloucester, Massachusetts, September 27, 1812, and died at Boston, December 31, 1880. Requiescat!

The destruction of the *Lusitania* has, of course, caused great excitement, and an anti-German feeling almost universal. There are now no neutrals and no pro-Germans, only Americans and Germans. President Wilson's message, delivered today, is firmer than was expected, and Germany will either comply with the American demands, paying an indemnity, apologising and promising to change her tactics of naval warfare, or find the United States in the field against her. And this will be a formidable matter, small as are our army and navy; we can send England much more ammunition than we are at present sending and also take possession of the German merchant vessels now in New York harbor. I enclose a poem from next Sunday's *Times*, which shows my attitude in the *Lusitania* affair. The torpedoing of an unarmed ship, carrying neutrals, certainly cannot be justified; it was an error as well as a crime.

You remember, I suppose, that I told you I was going to go in for fiction. I have started in. I took a story called "Try a Tin Today!" to a literary agent this morning.

It must be exciting to be in England, but the United States is exciting enough itself, nowadays. Feeling is as high as it was during the days preceding the Spanish-American War. I think that the effect of America's entrance into the hostilities will be to hasten the coming of peace.

I hope you find the Fauconberg Arms comfortable. Drink plenty of Bass—good Heavens, think of Bass at sixpence—when I pay .30 for a drink, Bass only in name!

You'll be having a birthday soon, now, won't you? Be a good infant and see what a present you'll get!

Yours affectionately, JOYCE.

1915

DEAR BRAT—I'm afraid you didn't like your birthday
poem! Your postcard about it seemed to show that you
didn't like it. It's a good poem, however, and I'll give you
another one when you come back, when you get your regular
birthday present.

I hope the letters I posted to you at Coxwold have been
forwarded to you at Buxton. Remember me to Mr. Smilter.

I am going lecturing in October—I sent you my lecture
circular, I think. I've already had offers from Cincinnati,
Chicago, Washington, Toronto, Sharon (Pennsylvania) and
Prairie du Chien (Wisconsin) and Buffalo.

I enclose a poem which I hope to sell to the magazine that
printed "The House With Nobody In It." My sonnet on
Rupert Brooke, which I sent you, will be in the New York
Bookman for September. I'll send you a copy. I sent you
a *Harper's Weekly* with my essay on "Sign-boards" recently.

I suppose Buxton is pleasantly busy after the quiet of
Coxwold. But don't drink those flat sulphurous waters—
drink ale! And when you get back, I'll take you to Farrish's
Chop House and we'll have some Burton ale.

Yours affectionately, JOYCE.

DEAR BRAT—I'm sorry you didn't like your poem; as a matter of fact, it's a good poem. But I'll give you another when you get back, when I give you your birthday present.

My father was out yesterday to Mahwah. He sails next Saturday. He seems well.

Aline's spoons must have gone down on the *Arabic*. She will value her ivory cross highly. I am glad you got it.

You remember the *Book News Monthly*, which printed Mrs. Byer's interview with me? I have a job reviewing poetry for it. I am to write four articles a year about all the new books of verse.

I hope to publish a book of essays soon. I find I have twenty-five on hand.

I am looking forward to your return and will, of course, meet the boat. I don't think there is much chance of a war before your return. But we must go to war sooner or later.

Yours affectionately, JOYCE.

————————

1915

DEAR BRAT—I don't know that this letter will reach England before you sail, but it may be forwarded to the boat. As I've already told you, you are to receive a new birthday poem when you return, as well as your birthday present.

That letter of yours about the hypothetical wounded man carrying his own head was a highly entertaining bit of description. You certainly can write letters!

As to my lectures, most of them will be out West. But I may have some in Montclair and Jersey City, and these I'll certainly give you an opportunity to attend.

You are an impudent infant, with your comments on my interview with Dr. Vizetelly!

I'll be very glad to have you back in a respectable country. The first Thursday after your return, we'll have luncheon at the Garret restaurant, where they have that excellent view over the harbor. And "Treasure Island" is to be played this year—we'll have to go to see it!

Yours affectionately, JOYCE.

DEAR BRAT—Glad you find Grimsby amusing. Canada's a nice place, but ridiculous confusion in money—American, English, Canadian—absurd. I repeat—hoping thereby to hurt the censor's feelings—absurd!

Hope you found the Hotel Statler in Buffalo comfortable. I think the Statler hotels are the best in the country—better value for the money than any New York hotels.

In a week or so I'm going out to Winona, Minnesota, to give a commencement address. And by the way, I have to wear a cap and gown—do you know where those garments are? I have an idea that they are in New Brunswick, but I don't remember seeing them there.

It's possible I'll be up towards Grimsby in July or August, if you're a good infant. I suppose my father keeps you supplied with newspapers and magazines, doesn't he? Let me know the names of any you wish sent.

We had the last Dickens Fellowship meeting of the season last night. Ellis Parker Butler read. It was pouring, so there wasn't much of a crowd.

Well, I'll write you again soon. By the way—this is very important—by all means drink Cosgrove's ale! It's made in Canada. You can't get it in the United States, and it's admirable—much better than the Bass you get over here. Be a good infant and drink large quantities of it.

Yours affectionately, JOYCE.

DEAR BRAT—I'm rather glad you're going to the Berk-shires. I thought you might find Grimsby dull. It's pleasant to have been in Canada, however. What part of the Berk-shires do you intend to go to? You might find it more amusing at Cape Cod. There are some nice places to stay at there.

It's a fact about its being bad for the eyes for anyone to shave his upper lip. You see, a man in shaving his upper lip focusses his eyes upon it, thus crossing them. And this inevitably has a weakening effect. And that's why artillery officers and I have moustaches.

I'm going back to New York at the end of this week. I have a lecture at Sinsinawa, Wisconsin, on Friday or Saturday.

I am glad to learn you are going to drink Cosgrove's ale. It is an admirable beverage.

Yours affectionately, JOYCE.

DEAR BRAT—Much obliged for letters and papers. My father found the academic cap and Aline believes the gown is in a box in our cellar. If I don't find it I can borrow one.

I'm going West the end of next week, giving an address at a college in Winona, Minnesota, a week from Monday, that is, the fifth of June. On the 10th of June I lecture at Sinsinawa, Wisconsin. The intervening days I expect to spend at Campion College, Prairie du Chien, Wisconsin, visiting some friends. That is the address you'd better put on any letters you send me the latter part of next week or the early part of the week following.

I am glad you find Grimsby comfortable, and earnestly urge that you drink Cosgrove's ale. On this side of the border it is impossible to obtain it. It is made in Toronto.

"Main Street" will be in *House and Garden* soon. I'll send you a copy.

I'm not going to Montreal this June, but I'll be at Cliff Haven, which is on Lake Champlain, in the northern part of New York State, in July, and I may run up to Grimsby then. I don't think it's a very long trip.

You ought to do some more writing while you are at Grimsby. I think you could have sold that "Cooking Dinner" story if you'd expanded it and sent it out to magazines a few more times. Sometimes a story goes to fifteen or twenty magazines before it is taken. I recently sold *The Argosy* a story called "Try a Tin Today!" that had been rejected by about a dozen magazines.

Edward Marshall has just returned from his exciting adventures abroad. He was on the *Sussex* when it was torpedoed, and the shock made him deaf. But he will probably recover his hearing.

Be a good infant and don't forget to drink Cosgrove's ale. I have about four books being published presently—essays, poems, and anthology, book of interviews, and a book of Belloc's poems for which I wrote a preface.

Yours affectionately, JOYCE.

DEAR BRAT—That was a very entertaining tragic letter you sent me today, or rather, that I received today. I guess you'll find Grimsby all right after you get used to it.

I read before the Federation of Women's Clubs yesterday, and Dr. Mary Walker was present. Have you ever heard of her? She wears a frock coat and trousers, being permitted to wear men's clothing by a special Act of Congress. She was a nurse in the Civil War.

I am growing a moustache to save my eyes. You know, shaving the upper lip is said to weaken one's vision—that is why all artillery officers are obliged to wear moustaches. If you don't believe me, ask an officer.

The mortar-board was in New Brunswick, and I found the gown down cellar out here. I leave for the West Saturday morning, and from the 5th to the 10th of June my address will be as I told you—Campion College, Prairie du Chien, Wisconsin.

In this envelope you will find a picture taken when I was in Cleveland some weeks ago. The dog is very good-looking, but he was unfortunate in not knowing how to pose for a photograph.

I am sending you by this mail a copy of *The Bellman*, containing a poem of mine called "The Proud Poet." I don't know whether or not you'll like it—it's a colloquial sort of a thing.

You have not yet replied to my inquiry as to Cosgrove's ale! Kindly give this matter your immediate attention!

Be a good infant and you may get a birthday present.

Yours affectionately, JOYCE.

Good Samaritan Hospital, Suffern, N. Y., 1916

DEAR BRAT—Thanks for excellent tobacco and pipe. My ribs are healing up rapidly, so the doctor says I'll be out of the hospital this week. I think the rest has done me good; this is a delightful place to stay, and commuting is hard in hot weather. I may take another week off after I leave the hospital.

My accident may make your birthday poem arrive a few days late, but you'll get it all right. Be a good infant, and you'll get nice birthday presents after you get back.

Yours affectionately, JOYCE.

Don't think of coming out here! I'll be out and probably back at Cliff Haven before you could get here.

––––––––

1916

DEAR BRAT—Enclosed you will find your birthday poem. I hope you like it; if you don't, tell me, and I'll write you another one.

I am out of the hospital now, and expect to go to my work in New York within a week. I am not going to Cliff Haven until later, so as to take in a celebration they have there, and also the wedding of some people we know.

The Ramapos, mentioned in the last line of this poem, are, you know, the hills around Mahwah.

I am glad you find Adams pleasant. You must take a motor ride to some of the deserted villages out toward Arlington, Vermont.

Be a good infant and drink cider. Musty ale is not a good drink; I got it mixed up with Burton ale, which is excellent.

Yours affectionately, JOYCE.

Mahwah, N. J., 1916

DEAR BRAT—It certainly is time I got a letter from you. I've had several postcards which seemed to indicate more or less violently, your departure from Canada. It must be nice to see Mt. Graylock, a most excellent mountain, as I remember it. You should take a motor trip up through the Notch to the Bellows Pipe, if possible, and also look up Dave Eddy, the original "Dave Lilly." I think you will find it very pleasant in the Berkshires, and hope Arthur's wife is as good a cook as his mother was. Is Arlington, Vermont, near where you are? I know some very nice people there, who sent us some excellent maple sugar and syrup recently.

I am going to Cliff Haven to lecture for the week beginning July 17, and after that I may go to the training camp at Plattsburg for a month. I think it will do me a lot of good to go to Plattsburg, and it will also be enjoyable.

I am now in my office, and find your address on a postcard, so this letter will reach you all right. But it certainly is time I got a letter from you!

According to this morning's paper, we are at war with Mexico, so the Plattsburg camp may be off. Might go to Mexico, instead, with young Michael.

Be a good infant and you'll get a good birthday poem.

Yours affectionately, JOYCE.

DEAR BRAT—Hope you don't mind being written to in pencil. It's impossible to go upstairs and get ink without disturbing thousands of young children. I am sending you herewith pictures of some of these young children. I will later have some pictures taken of Rose giving a tea—she sits out at a little table in a tent I recently bought and serves imaginary tea in the excellent tea-set you sent her. The tea-set, being of tin, can be left out all night, and even given to Deborah to play with, without danger of the destruction of it.

I am going to Cliff Haven, on Lake Champlain, on July 17th, to lecture at the Summer School. By the way, the men standing beside me in the picture I sent you are priests—neither of them is a layman. We are on our way to the Mississippi to go for a ride in the motor-boat. It certainly is nice out in Prairie du Chien. I really think you'd like the Middle West better than the East, and I know you'd like Chicago better than any other great city, except London. It is not in the least like New York, and its hotels are absolutely heavenly. I am a good judge of hotels, as you, having been to the Statler, are aware.

I am glad you are enjoying Adams. It must be fine to see Mt. Graylock again. Remember me to Arthur. We enjoyed much your entertaining description of the humours associated with the local tragedy.

Yours affectionately, JOYCE.

DEAR BRAT—Thanks very much for excellent pajamas, or, in the British manner, pyjamas. I needed them. Much obliged. Kenton likes his suits, and will himself write to thank you. He is teaching Rose her catechism. A few mornings ago he was dressing, and Rose was sitting on the bed. It was about half past seven. Kenton asked the first question in the catechism, which is, "Who made you?" Rose answered the question correctly, but without enthusiasm. Then Kenton asked the second question, "What is Man?" Whereupon Rose threw herself forward until her head rested on her knees, and said weakly: "O, Kenton, I'm dying! Don't ask me any more!" So Kenton stopped teaching her the catechism until after breakfast.

I took up so much time with my week at Cliff Haven lecturing, and my month at the hospital and at home, that I won't be able to stay away from my office any more this summer. Otherwise I'd try to get up to Adams.

I will send you a copy of *Punch* containing my essay "The Booklover," which you will read with more equanimity than that with which you regarded "The Bally Pub." Your old friend, Louis Wetmore, came out here while I was laid up, and bitterly reproved me for writing disrespectfully of musty ale, a beverage which he says I drank with enthusiasm when we were in London.

Say, today, I suddenly saw your birthday present in a shop on Fifth Avenue! It is a very large present, and very nice— the nicest you've had! You'll receive it as soon as you get back.

Be a good infant, and drink Hinchcliffe's ale, and Evans' pale ale, but not Evans' Indian ale.

Yours affectionately, JOYCE.

DEAR BRAT—Glad you are enjoying Adams. Did you get the copy of *Punch* I sent you, containing "The Booklover"? When are you coming home? A very good place to eat is the Park Avenue Hotel, which has a very large fountain·in its dining room.

By the way, I forgot to tell you that when I was laid up with broken ribs, the things that I read most frequently, and with the greatest enjoyment, were the bound volumes of *Punch*, and the volumes of Leech's drawings. You brought them to me from England a few years ago, and I think they're the best present I ever received. Their humour wears admirably.

I find myself about to vote for a Republican candidate for president. I expected to vote for Roosevelt, but in default of him I'll vote for Hughes. The Mexican situation alone is sufficient to make me vote against Wilson.

I am glad you are keeping up your croquet. Why don't you have a croquet field made at New Brunswick? There is plenty of room in the side yard.

I'll be glad to see you, and you'll get a very nice birthday present. Yours affectionately, JOYCE.

DEAR BRAT—Of course I'd be glad to see you in N. Y. You could stop at the Savoy. But the only free time I have is 12 to 2, and I generally have errands then, so it wouldn't be worth while coming. We leave for the South August 5. Thanks for the toilet case just received. Eagerly await hussif. Soon fed by U. S. A. I hear it's very nice in Spartanburg, S.C. Good swimming there. You'll get birthday poem soon, perhaps. If you don't like it, return it and get another. All goods returnable. I hope you don't call soldiers Sammies. Disgusting nickname. Yours affectionately, JOYCE.

En Route Chicago, June 12, 1917

DEAR BRAT—Got a very nice letter from you this morning. Glad you like Fr. O'Connor. Also glad you'll be back on the 18th of June. We'll go to Healy's Golden Glades, a very amusing place.

I am making a flying trip to Prairie du Chien, Wisconsin, to give the Baccalaureate address at Campion College. I expect to get back to Larchmont on Sunday morning. It's a big trip just to give one address, but I made the engagement last February and didn't want to break it. Also I greatly enjoy visiting Campion—it is a beautiful place, and the people there are very nice. This will be my fourth visit to the college.

The children are all well and Michael is very elastic—when you punch his stomach your fist bounds back as from a punching bag. It is excellent exercise. I am going to teach it to Deborah; I think it will be helpful in developing her upper arms.

I have not yet heard about my anthology, but I think George H. Doran will publish it. He has accepted "Main Street and Other Poems"—how do you like the title?

When our lease expires in October I think we'll take another house in Larchmont—near where we are now, but closer to the Sound.

Yours affectionately, JOYCE.

236

DEAR BRAT—I got your very amusing letter on my return from the West, where I had a fine time. My Baccalaureate address delivered at Campion is to be printed as a pamphlet. I'll send you some copies. I may have copies of it next week when you are in town. Also I may have my poetry prize medal then. I don't expect to go to camp until about July 15th, but after July 1st, I may be on duty in New York at the Armory.

I am going to write an article that will amuse you—about Alfred Watts, the imaginary poet Margaret Widemer and I created.

Isn't it exciting about Dr. Condon and New Brunswick? Do you remember him? I remember seeing him ride past the house.

We'll have a lot of fun next week.

Yours affectionately, JOYCE.

July 10, 1917

DEAR BRAT—If you desire I will send you a number of circulars like the one enclosed.

The Seventh stays at the Armory after next Sunday, and then in about ten days goes to a training camp, probably in South Carolina. I'll send you the address as soon as I know it accurately. I find I'll have to get a lot of stuff to take to camp with me—I only learned what I would need last night. Will you please give me an order on Rogers Peet, 34th Street store, or telegraph it (not signing the telegram "Gerber") to get some truck—chiefly hussifs and towels and similar things?

Received a very amusing letter from you recently. Glad to know my judgment as to the appropriate wrist for watches was correct. The one you got me is excellent and keeps good time. Much obliged! Yours affectionately, JOYCE.

1917

Dear Brat—I think I'll get my father to send you some stamped and addressed envelopes to use in writing me! The enclosed envelope was posted in Pittsfield with a one cent stamp, and I had to send another one cent stamp to Pittsfield to get it! If I'd done a thing like that—

I'm going to Prairie du Chien soon for a commencement address, but I have to take the train right back after it because of drill. We were on guard in the Armory all day, expecting a riot call, but none came. We expect to go to training camp July 15th.

Be a good infant and you'll get a nice birthday present. Aline, Michael, Kenton, Rose and Deborah send love.

Yours affectionately, Joyce.

1917

Dear Brat—Enclosed letter may amuse you, especially the part about the deserted grandsons. Entertaining thing to do. Aline and I think of shipping Kenton and Michael, not to speak of Christopher, to Cheshire. By the way, Christopher does not mean "cross-bearer," but "Christ-bearer," which is something else again. I gave Mrs. Sillcocks desired information. I hope no other aspiring authors have infantile photographs of me. I go to the Armory to stay Sunday, but I'll have time off frequently to go home and to the office. I don't know when we'll go to training camp; perhaps in August, perhaps in September. I am engaged on an anthology of Catholic poems, to be published September 1st; have to finish it this week. Wrist watch keeps good time and enjoys resting Melvolina.

Yours affectionately, Joyce.

238

1917

DEAR BRAT—Do you know that in addition to being worn on the left wrist, a soldier's wrist-watch should be turned so that the face is parallel to the palm, not the back, of the hand? No hussif yet received! Very soon I'll be in camp, and ready to receive such things as boxes of cigars, cans of tobacco, cans (or, if you prefer, tins) of ginger snaps, and pipes and such things.

I passed my Federal physical examination yesterday, and tomorrow all the Regiment is mustered into Federal service. I drill about four hours a day, and also have guard duty and such things. I didn't get to the office today, but expect to do so tomorrow. There will probably be a letter from you there. When I come back from the war I don't think I'll go back on the *Times;* I think I'll get a department on some magazine and spend more time lecturing.

Be a good infant and you'll get a nice birthday present.

Yours affectionately, JOYCE.

———————— 1917

DEAR BRAT—Presently you'll get a telegram from me, sent collect, if you don't look out! I've sent you two letters and got only one! Write! But I got a postcard and two telegrams, and also a telegram from my father telling me to write. From your telegram I'm glad to learn you received my letters. Ridiculous. Nevertheless, you'll get a very nice birthday present from me this year. And we'll have a lot of fun when you come back at the end of June. We'll go to Healy's Golden Glades—a very amusing place.

I have written four articles for "Warner's Library of the World's Best Literature"—the articles being on Masefield, Cawein, William Vaughn Moody and Francis Thompson. Louis Wetmore has just come in and sends you his love. He has enlisted in the 7th, too. Yours affectionately, JOYCE.

1917

Dear Brat—Thanks for order. on Rogers Peet. Got several things there today—safety razor, bag, etc. They didn't have hussifs. If you find any, you might send me one. Address me at *Times* until I give you my new address. I may find out tonight where I'll be stationed. I think we'll be in New York at the Armory for a month yet, but I'm not sure. Have to go on the wagon Sunday, when we are mobilised. Terrible, isn't it? Also, we can't smoke on the streets when we are in uniform, and we are always to be in uniform!

Yours affectionately, Joyce.

1917

Dear Brat—I haven't heard from you since you left N. Y., but there may be a letter at the office. I haven't been there recently—I've been too busy at the Armory. For the last twenty-four hours I've been on guard duty—two hours on and four hours off. By the way, I'm supposed, you know, to have become much thinner since I joined the army. Well, I got weighed yesterday and the scales showed 178 pounds— only two pounds less than I weighed last winter! So either I've not lost fat or I've gained muscle.

If, or when, my transfer to the 69th goes through, my address will be Private Joyce Kilmer, Company K, 165th Regiment, Camp Mills, Mineola, Garden City, Long Island, New York. You see, or rather don't, that the 69th is now the 165th. But I'll let you know when, or if, the transfer occurs.

That certainly is a fine pipe you bought me. I'm enjoying it daily. I hope you got your bag. Let me know if you didn't and I'll send you another poem.

Yours affectionately, Joyce.

DEAR BRAT—Sorry to be so long in writing to you, but I am spending most of my time since Monday at the Armory, and have had no time to do any writing. I drill about five hours a day, and have guard duty and other things like that to attend to. I guess I must have lost about 10 pounds this week. It's terribly hot, and we still wear our winter uniforms—woolen breeches and woolen shirts. We expect to go to training camp at Spartanburg, South Carolina, about August 5. We are not yet all mustered into Federal service, and expect to have the Federal physical examination tomorrow. Then we'll be mustered in. The Federal physical examination is stricter than the State examination, which I passed when I enlisted, April 23, but I expect to pass this all right, as I must be in better shape than when I enlisted. All this week we've been at the Armory from 9 A. M. to 4:30 P. M., and sometimes later. I was one of the detail from the 7th that went to General Austen's funeral and fired a volley over his grave.

I told you, I think, about the Catholic anthology I'm trying to finish up. I hope to be able to work at it Sundays when I'm in camp.

As to hussifs, they are what you Americans call housewifes', or rather housewives', field sewing kits; in other words, you get them at department stores and Rogers Peet doesn't carry them.

You'll get a birthday present and a poem if you are good.

Yours affectionately, JOYCE.

DEAR BRAT—Enclosed find copies of the two sonnets that won the prizes I mentioned in a recent letter. "The Annunciation" won first prize, and "The Visitation" second, as I told you. I've asked the magazine to give second prize to some one else.

My new book "Main Street and Other Poems" will be published September 1st. I have just signed the contract.

What time in June will you be back? I'll be in New York until the last day of the month, but my Monday and Friday evenings are taken up by drill, so be back on some other evening and we'll go to Healy's "Golden Glades," which is the most magnificent cabaret ever made.

Yours affectionately, JOYCE.

DEAR BRAT—I have no copy of your birthday poem, but will try to rewrite it from memory, and if I can't, I'll write another one for you, and perhaps you'll like it better. I'll give it to you—the old or the new one—when I see you this week. Constance's wedding is next Thursday at 8:30 at the National Arts Club. I am to lead the bride up the aisle and hand her to Mr. Alden, who will give her away. It will be a military wedding, as the groom has just been commissioned Captain. Constance is not sending out any invitations, only announcements. She is very glad you are coming! We will have a lot of fun. I suppose you'll come on Wednesday and stay until Sunday, won't you?

I'm sorry I had to get back to the Armory so soon the last day you were in New York. We certainly are working hard these days. But it's a very interesting life.

Yours affectionately, JOYCE.

1917

DEAR BRAT—When I go to training camp still is uncertain. The Seventh Regiment takes part in a farewell parade of New York on Thursday of this week, but it may not leave for a week after that. Then again it may leave next day—but probably not. As you know, I am being transferred to the 69th (now called the 165th). The transfer has not yet gone through, but it may this week. It is certain to go through in the course of time. Then I'll go to training camp at Mineola, N. Y., instead of at Spartanburg, South Carolina. I'll let you know when I myself know.

Your letter was highly entertaining, especially the reported conversation. Amusing critter. Send you another birthday poem soon. Regimental drill this afternoon, so I find it hard to write. Be a good infant and by all means have cinnamon toast for your tea.

Yours affectionately, JOYCE.

Headquarters Company, 165th U. S. Infantry,
American Expeditionary Forces, November 12, 1917

DEAR BRAT—My fountain pen doesn't work well, so perhaps you won't mind being typewritten to this time. We are arriving today, all in excellent health and spirits. I hope to be able to cable to Timpson to cable to you of my arrival, but do not know whether or not I shall be able to do so.

I'll be glad to receive some envelopes addressed to you, as I may have some difficulty in obtaining plain envelopes. The Y. M. C. A. supplies the soldiers with free stationery, but it is all covered with American flags and things. The last lot of groceries you mentioned did not reach me before my departure, but it has probably been forwarded from the camp and will undoubtedly come in handy over here. It's pretty cold and damp this morning, but I believe it will be pleasanter and healthier than Camp Mills.

Your friend, Father Duffy, would send his love if he knew I were writing to you. He has been doing the work of about twenty chaplains, but seems to thrive on it. Yesterday afternoon he held a service for Protestants, and I typewrote some hymns for distribution—"Jesus, Lover of My Soul," "Nearer, my God to Thee," "Onward, Christian Soldiers" and the like. The service was well attended and the daily masses have been crowded.

Aline must have had a hard time with the children having whooping-cough. I hope that they are well over it by now, but I am afraid that they are not, for I remember the ailment as lasting for a month or so.

When you see Mrs. Corbin tell her that I greatly enjoyed the chocolate cake she sent me. It arrived in excellent condition. I'll write to thank her very soon—possibly today. If she wants to know what to send me over here, you might suggest copies of *The Century*, *Scribner's*, and other magazines, and if she wants to send books you might tell her that I have at present a great desire for paper-bound copies of the works of Wilkie Collins. Also, anyone sending Christmas boxes to soldiers should do so at once.

You'll get your Christmas present this year, but it may be a little late. Be a good infant!

Yours affectionately, JOYCE.

Headquarters Co., 165th Inf.,
A. E. F., France, January 13, 1918

DEAR BRAT—I have not had a letter from you since Christmas Eve, but I believe there is a bunch of mail awaiting me at a nearby station, and I expect it tonight or tomorrow. Yesterday I got a very fine package from you containing six glasses of admirable jelly and a box of chocolate covered nuts. Much obliged! Sweet stuff like that is what I desire above everything else now. That and cigars. Also I received from John Timpson & Co. $100.00 in American Express Cheques, and $9.50 from the 7th Regiment, back pay, and a fountain pen from my Council of the Knights of Columbus. A pretty good haul!

This town is rather like some of the English villages you love so much. I think you would enjoy a trip through France some time, but probably not this winter. However, I am comfortable enough, and can do without an afternoon nap and cream on my shredded wheat.

I enjoy your letters tremendously; and am looking forward to getting a batch of them tomorrow. I wish I could write half as interestingly.

Yours affectionately, JOYCE.

Headquarters Co., 165th Inf.,
A. E. F., France, January 31, 1918

DEAR BRAT—In the course of a day or so you should receive one of the Aime Dupont pictures I had taken last August
or September.   They are not particularly good, but they are
the only pictures in uniform I have had taken.   Aime Dupont
sent them to me at Camp Mills, and they were forwarded to
me out here.

I received a second box from Finley-Acker, containing
excellent jelly and much candy.   From my father I have received several boxes of cigars, as well as $200.00.   I hope he
received my letter of thanks.

Your letters come, not regularly, of course; that is not to
be expected these days, but in bunches three or four days apart.
Judging by the numbers I am getting them all.   It is a great
pleasure to hear from you so frequently, and you certainly
can write letters worth reading.   I wish I could write half as
interestingly.

I think you will enjoy a trip through rural France after
the war is over.   You will find it very much like the parts
of England you like best—in architecture, landscape, people.

I was very much interested in hearing that Maurice Kane
is coming over as a Y.M.C.A. worker.   As you know, I am
not exactly a Y.M.C.A. enthusiast, but what they are doing
for the troops over here in the way of selling American tobacco
and cakes, and furnishing writing and reading rooms is very
good, and most, if not all, the men in the work are over the
age when they could be good soldiers, or have some physical
disqualification; so I don't think any the less of Maurice for
going into the work, but it is amusing considering his High
Church ideas.

By the way, and "why," you ask, "do you say by the
way," read "Monksbride," by John Ayscough.   I think it is

247

published by Dodd, Meade Co. Or, if you don't want to buy
it, Aline will loan it to you.

I suppose you have read the new Sherlock Holmes book?
Admirable! I enjoyed it as much as I enjoy his earlier stuff.

It is getting to be much pleasanter out here with the coming
of spring. I imagine it must be delightful in the summer.

I think that my father's plan for sending you to San
Francisco for the spring and summer is excellent. By all
means do it.

I have not yet received the additional envelopes you spoke
of. The name of my anthology, concerning which you in-
quire, is "Dreams and Images"—Anthology of Catholic
Verse, and the publishers are Boni & Liveright.

Yours affectionately, JOYCE.

DEAR BRAT—Got a very delightful letter from you today from Lakewood. I am glad you enjoyed your stay there. The sweater arrived, and it certainly is a magnificent specimen of knitting, and the wristlets are wonderfully purled, whatever purling may be. Probably I shall need both sweater and wristlets for many weeks, for although it is spring now, it often is cold. Much obliged!

Under separate cover I am sending you my warrant as Sergeant. I thought you might like to have it to frame and hang in the Old-fashioned Room. The "draft" in the corner means that the Regiment was drafted into Federal Service; that is, made a part of the United States Army instead of a part of the New York State National Guard.

I suppose you have read in the newspapers of the Regiment's recent activities. Now we are taking it easy in a very pleasant little town. I hope we may stay here at least a month, as it is hard to work when the Regiment is moving about the country. I had a week's respite from office work some time ago, and spent it doing what is called observation work for the Regimental Intelligence Section. It was most interesting.

Did Aline tell you of Kenton's success in school? It seems that he won a gold medal for being the best pupil in the school. I was delighted to learn it. So nearly as I can remember, I was not an especially keen student when I was his age, although I became one later.

There is practically no chance of my rising any higher in the Regiment than Sergeant, and I am perfectly content. To become an officer, I would have to go to school away from the Regiment for several months, then if I failed to pass my examination and win a commission, I would be sent to some other regiment than this, and if I succeeded I would be sent as an officer, not back to the 69th, but to some other outfit. I want very much to stay with the Regiment; I have many good friends here, and I would feel lost in any other military organization.

I am looking forward to receiving the photographs you have had taken. They must be fine. By this time you probably have received the one I sent you. I hope you like it.

I hope that the meatless, wheatless day hysteria has passed. It was a foolish idea, of no possible value to the country, and potentially harmful.

Your letters are very gratefully received, and I am looking forward eagerly to receiving the cake and candy you mention. Everything else you have written of in your letters has arrived in good condition, and a day or two ago I got five big jars of excellent tobacco from the Dickens Fellowship. A most intelligent gift.

Yours affectionately, JOYCE.

Headquarters Co., 165th Inf.,
A. E. F., France, April 18, 1918

DEAR BRAT—The sweater arrived a few days ago, and I certainly was glad to get it. It is a fine garment, beautiful to look at and most comfortably warm, and the touch of red is delightfully characteristic. Much obliged!

I have not heard from you, nor from any one in the States for about two weeks, but tomorrow or next day six truck loads of mail will be left at Regimental Headquarters, and there surely will be several letters from you. We get our mail in big lots. For about two weeks we have been receiving packages and no letters. I received the candy, of which I spoke at length in a recent letter, and which I remember with enthusiasm, and a number of newspapers from my father, and some *Saturday Evening Posts* from you. I greatly enjoyed the story you praised, "Call for Mr. Keefe." I interviewed its author, Ring Lardner, when I was last in Chicago. I do not think that the interview appears in my book.

And speaking of my book, let me renew my inquiries about my anthology, "Dreams and Images." Why does not some one send me a copy? I have asked Aline, but in vain. I should think the publishers would be sending me a copy, but I have received none from them. I don't ask you to send me one; when you are minded to send anything, let it be candy —box after box, but much cheap candy rather than a little costly, but I shall be grateful if you will remind Aline to send me a copy. She must have received many of them from the publishers.

I am enjoying this town greatly, and wish I could tell you its name. There is a little river near here, and this afternoon I had a swim. The water was pretty cold, but it was good to get a real wash and to splash around a little. It is getting nice and warm now—a great relief for all of us.

251

I am glad you enjoyed your stay in Lakewood. I enjoyed the fruits of it in the form of those two magnificent boxes of candy.

I hope you make a trip to California. It will do you a lot of good and be a fine experience to remember.

I am enclosing a letter from John Timpson & Co., which you will please give to my father. It relates to an insurance application which he wanted to make for me. He asked me to cable to him about it. I didn't have any money, so I wrote to John Timpson Co., and had them cable. The allusion in the letter to the prospect of seeing me, is the result of a statement in my letter to the effect that I might go to England on my leave. I expect to have seven days' leave soon, but I am afraid I will not be allowed to leave France.

I am looking forward to receiving your photograph soon, and some letters.

Be a good child, and go to see "The Copperhead" and tell me how you like it.

Yours affectionately, JOYCE.

DEAR BRAT—Do not be alarmed at the multiplicity of requests enclosed The reason is that, as you are aware, packages can no longer be mailed or expressed to soldiers serving in France except at their request, approved by their Regimental, or higher, commander. So I have had the enclosed list typed and approved. The system is this: You desire to send me some cigars, let us say. If you merely address a box of cigars to me it will not be taken by the postal authorities, but if you show the receiving clerk in the post office or some other authorised person, the enclosed duly approved request, you will find that he will accept the package for transmittal. That is the use for which the slips are intended. They are not meant to be requests requiring immediate attention.

I have asked to be relieved from my statistical work, and expect to be out of the office by Monday; today is Saturday. I am going into the Intelligence Section, which is much more interesting work than I have been doing. I expect to keep my rank of Sergeant, but I would be willing to do it even if I had to become a Private. My work in the Intelligence Section is that of observer, for which my newspaper work has given me some preparation.

I hear that a load of mail has arrived, so I probably shall receive a letter from you before evening, I am glad to say. Yesterday I got a copy of the *Saturday Evening Post* from you, and I certainly was glad to see it.

In one of your recent letters your account of your verbal battle with one of the musical —— amused me very much, not only because "we stay-at-homes" seemed to me to be excellent satire, but also because I have a vivid recollection of being "done" by a musical —— for concert tickets some fifteen years ago. However, I paid him eventually, and I shouldn't hold a grudge against him. If I held a grudge against every one who has "done" me since that time, I'd have a scruge-like existence indeed. But I can't help enjoying having him so neatly and completely crushed.

It's nice and warm now, a pleasant relief after a severe winter. Some days ago I went in swimming in a river near here; it was very enjoyable, and yesterday I had a shower bath. It's fine to be within reach of such a luxury.

I wonder where you will spend your summer? Probably not in Canada, after your experience there last summer. I think you probably would do well to try the Adirondacks this time. So far as I can remember, you have never been there, and there is a good deal about it you would like.

By the way, the young man you met in Henri's was not an officer, but a non-commissioned officer like myself, only some grades higher, since you say he was a Sergeant-Major, and the number of his regiment indicates that he is a drafted man. Enough of him. However, some of the drafted men are very nice fellows.

I am going to have some postcard photographs taken in a nearby town as soon as I acquire the requisite ten francs, which will be soon, and I will send you several (not francs, but photographs), also you will get your belated valentine soon.

Yours affectionately, JOYCE.

Headquarters Co., 165th Inf.,
A. E. F., France, May 18, 1918

DEAR BRAT—Under separate cover I am sending you a couple of postcard photographs which will amuse you. I like them better than the picture in uniform I had taken in the States.

As to your "War Mother" poem, I hesitate to tell you how much I like it, because I'm afraid you will think I am trying to flatter you. It certainly is the best poem you ever wrote—beautiful, original and well sustained. I have seen no recent war verse I like so well. There is no question but what you will sell it to some good magazine. I certainly congratulate you, and congratulate the magazine fortunate enough to print your poem.

I am very glad to hear of the deserved success your songs met at Lakewood, and in general of your triumphs at the Dickens Fellowship and elsewhere. I wish I could have witnessed them, but I will be seeing more of the same sort next winter. That is what we like to hear about over here—triumphs and celebrations, and in general, the pleasant and prosperous course of civilised life. Of course, we soldiers are undergoing hardships and privations. We expect to. But we don't spend our time advertising them. But in the States when they find they must do without quite so much wheat, or meat, or something of the sort, instead of just going without and keeping their mouths shut, they advertise their remarkable abstention by having "wheatless days" and "meatless days" and all that sort of hysterical rubbish, and filling the papers with the news, thereby disgusting us soldiers and undoubtedly comforting the enemy. I think I'll start a strawberry ice-cream sodaless day for the Army; it would be just as sensible as what the people at home have been doing. If you (I don't mean you personally, of course) have to eat hardtack instead of butter-raised biscuit, why, eat the hardtack and shut up about it, but don't be such an ass as to have a butter-raised biscuitless Monday. And don't shut down on theatrical amusements, and don't deprive people of their honest drink. Merely making stay-at-homes dismal does not help the soldiers a bit. England's early "Business as Usual" scheme was more practical, and this is something of a concession for me to make.

There is quite a sermon on economics for you. Kindly read it to my father, whom it will edify and instruct. A recent letter from him shows that he utterly misunderstands my point of view on this subject, the result of lamentable careless reading by him of one of my letters, in which I contrasted the sanity and common sense of the French through years of tragic poverty, starvation and ruin with the hysterical wail which a little self-denial brought from the States.

I am now having a delightful rest on top of a forest-covered mountain. I had a month of very hard and exciting work, the nature of which you can imagine, and now I have a fortnight's rest in ideal surroundings, and working only six hours out of every twenty-four, and that work is light and interesting.

Be a good infant, and send me your picture soon. No order is needed now.

Yours affectionately, JOYCE.

Headquarters Co., 165th Inf.,
A. E. F., France, May 27, 1918

DEAR BRAT—Your picture has come and I certainly am glad to have it. I think it is by far the best picture you have had taken. You look about eighteen! That is a delightful costume. But you must send another copy of the picture to Larchmont for framing, since in order to carry this with me it will be necessary to remove it from the mount.

I suppose by this time you have received the humourous photographs of myself I sent you.

I am delighted to know of the Kilburn Hall project. By all means buy the Hall; it will be an excellent investment. Property is now very cheap in England and prices will rise as soon as the war is over. I hope to be able to spend my summers in France after the war, and I have the place in mind—only about a day's run from London. I am absolutely in love with France, its people, its villages, its mountains, everything about it. America would do well to copy its attitude in the war. It has suffered tremendous hardships with dignity and humour, and kept its sanity and faith. America, to judge by the papers, grows hysterical over a little self-denial. Can't do without an extra lump of sugar in its tea without a band and speeches, and a sugarless Sunday. It's funny and rather pathetic to us soldiers, but I honestly think, although it may seem conceited to say so, that when we soldiers get back from the war we'll do the spiritual and intellectual life of the States a lot of good. France has taught us lessons of infinite value.

I am having an absolutely heavenly time since I joined the Intelligence Section. I wouldn't change places with any soldier of any rank in any outfit. This suits me better than any job I ever had in civil life. It certainly was fortunate I left the 7th.

As you know, the order about having written and approved requests for packages has been repealed, so let nothing deter you. The cake is not yet here. I will soak it in wine all right; don't worry about that. Speaking of wine, enclosed find some flowers given me by a very nice wineshop girl in a city near here.

"Madelon" is a perfectly respectable song, but Madelon is not a gun or anything else of the sort; it's the name of a girl who serves wine to the soldiers, as the song clearly states.

Read Eden Philpott's "Old Delaboll," a delightful tale of Cornish life.

Yours affectionately, JOYCE.

DEAR BRAT—I am enclosing two poems which I think you will like. "Rouge Bouquet" is to appear in *Scribner's* for July or August. A friend of mine, Emmet Watson, of ours, made a magnificent drawing for it, which I hope will accompany it in the magazine. The "Peace-Maker" I have just this hour completed, and I have not yet decided where to send it; probably to the *London New Witness*.

Tomorrow I expect to send you two other poems: one your long delayed valentine, the other a long more or less topical thing about a hike, which I think you will enjoy setting to music. It introduces at intervals songs that we sing during long marches.

There is a chance that I will be able to go to England on several days' leave in a few weeks. In that case I shall probably spend most of my time in London, with a possible visit to Oxfordshire, where my friend Mrs. Denis Eden lives.

I wish there was something I could do for you to expedite the purchase of Kilburn Hall, but since the Archbishop of York is in the States, you should yourself be able to make a deal with him. English real estate is a wise investment these days. It will go up fifty per cent. in a year's time. I wish I could afford to buy some property in this country. I certainly would like to live here. If the States go dry I honestly think I'll move my family over here; I can write for American papers without living in America. Then, if you move to Kilburn Hall I will be only a day's trip away from you, and you will love rural France almost as much as you love rural England.

I believe no packages can be sent from the States to soldiers in France. They can, however, be sent from England.

Be a good infant and learn to sing "Madelon."

Yours affectionately, JOYCE.

(The last letter received from Joyce)

Headquarters Co., 165th Inf.,
A. E. F., France, June 28, 1918

DEAR BRAT—I received three letters from you yesterday and today, the first I have had for a long time. Your letters always come in bunches like that, and this morning I received two admirable boxes of Mirror candy, in perfect condition. I certainly was delighted to get it, as it is a long time since I have had any candy. My gratitude is so great that I even will refer to it as "Sweets." I was also glad to get your picture taken on shipboard. You must send to Larchmont another copy of the picture of yourself looking at my photograph, you sent me some weeks ago, as I had to remove it from its mount and cut it down to make it fit into my wallet.

All the rest of the fellows in the Intelligence Section (there are nine of us, nearly all college graduates and men of some standing—editors, brokers, etc.) have pictures of their mothers, but none of them so good looking as mine. You would be amused at some of the scenes when your picture is exhibited. Tired from a long hike from a stay in the trenches, I am having an omelet and some fried potatoes and some vin rouge beaucop in a French peasant's little kitchen. It is a cottage such as you and I often visited in Derbyshire and Cambridgeshire— a low grey stone building with rose trees against the wall; a tiny garden and a geometrically neat path. The kitchen floor is of stone; the table is without a cloth, but shining from much polishing. The only thing to distinguish it from the typical English rural cottage is the crucifix on the wall and the wooden shoes at the door. (People wear sabots out-of-doors, cloth slippers in the house, leather shoes on Sunday.) After such a repast as I have described I take out my wallet to pay my bill, and the sharp eyes of little Marie or Pierre intently watching this strange soldat Americain, spy the picture. At once an inquisitive but delighted infant is on my knee demanding a closer inspection of the picture. Then mama must see it, and grandpere, and veuve vatre from across the street (the man of the house can't see it; he is away from home on the errand that brought me across the sea). Well, they all say "elle est jolie ma foi et jeune aussi." These comments have been made on your picture many times, in many towns, which I will one day show you on a map of France.

I have not much anxiety for my father, for I look on his condition as a state of rest really necessary to a mind so constantly busy, but I am glad that from you I have inherited the power of readily escaping from worry and work and entering with enthusiasm into whatever mirth I find around me— in finding good and true and merry friends everywhere. I think that some of this quality would have helped my father very much and increased his bodily and mental health. I worried grievously about you for a while, and wished that I could have been with you when my father was taken ill, but I don't worry now; you are too spirited and courageous for anybody to worry about. I certainly admire you more than ever, and look forward eagerly to regular banquets at Henri's and Rector's with you.

I want you to meet all the Regimental Intelligence Section —a fine bunch of men and good comrades. We have taken big chances together, and it has made us the best of friends. You will like them and they will like you.

Yours affectionately, JOYCE.

NOTES

Introduction

1. Armistice Day was November 11, 1918. In recent years its meaning has been broadened, and it has been renamed Veterans Day.
2. Sarah Coerr, as Sarah Flagler Cary, was teaching French and German at Rutgers Preparatory School during the period that Joyce Kilmer and Aline Murray were students there. Dad, I know, studied both languages under her, but I don't know about Mother's language studies there. Somehow, Sarah Flagler got condensed into Sf.

Chapter 1. Celebrating Individuals, Enjoying Differences

1. Netty or Nettie (I only remember her name from hearing it) was a black cook (and sometimes general houseworker) for my grandparents' over many years. I don't think I ever knew her last name. Mary Armstrong was her successor, also serving for many years.
2. In a letter to his mother, dated from Mahwah in 1916, Dad identifies the original, pictured in this poem, as Dave Eddy. The letter is on page 232.
3. The poem, "Martin" is written in Dad's notebook, in my possession, under the title, "Baldwin." A letter from Dad to his mother, identifying the original as a co-worker named Baldwin, is on page 192. Faith Baldwin, poet and novelist (now Faith Baldwin Cuthrell), is the daughter of that Stephen Charles Baldwin. My mother has told me that Dad and she sponsored Faith Baldwin's application to the Poetry Society of America.

Chapter 2. Delight in Food

1. When I was a student at Holy Cross College, Worcester, MA, a distinguished visitor chatting with me, remarked, "I bet you can't guess what my favorite Joyce Kilmer poem is." I suddenly knew for certain, and replied confidently, "Delicatessen." Many years later, when I was applying for my Library of Congress job, and went to ask Joseph P. Tumulty to recommend me, he told me that poem was *his* favorite. Some dozen years ago, I delighted in reading it to students at Bethune-Cookman College in Florida. After reading it, I realized that I should have made an introductory explanation to the effect that "delicatessen" was the long form of what many of them knew only as "deli."

Chapter 3. Tracing Relationships and Friendships Through Time

1. Cigars, pipes, and tobacco are mentioned so often in Dad's letters to his mother that I have generally refrained from indexing them.
2. "My mother's mother" is Elizabeth Turner Foster, and "my dead child" is Rose Kilburn Kilmer.
3. "For the Birthday of a Middle-Aged Child" was a birthday present sent to me at Georgetown Preparatory School, March 21, 1925. I

suppose sixteen *is* a sort of middle age for a child. It's a present I still cherish.

4. Rose's birthday was November 15, and Deborah's November 13. While Rose lived, we celebrated a joint birthday for them. I think this poem was written after Rose's death, and is about Deborah.

5. "Atonement" is sometimes taken to be a poem mourning Dad's death, but it was written and sent to him when he was with the A.E.F. in France. It is his *absence*, not his death, that she is mourning.

Chapter 4. Reading and Writing and Poem Reciting

1. The subject of "In Memory" is not identified, but I am of the opinion that she is Elizabeth Barrett Browning.

Chapter 5. Poetry: Fun and Fury

1. In 1911, when Richard Barham Middleton, an English poet, committed suicide in Brussels, many other young poets, in many countries, were overwhelmed with sentimental and romantic admiration. My mother told me that, when Dad gave out this poem about the man and the event at a meeting of the Poetry Society of America, there was an uproar.

Chapter 7. Disappointments—and a Glad Surprise

1. I don't know for sure, but I like to think that I, myself, may have been the "kilted Hedonist" from whose play Dad drew this spiritual lesson.

Chapter 12. Our Mahwah House and Neighborhood

1. The line, "Whenever I walk to Suffern along the Erie track," brings to mind the combination of religious fervor and practical sense typical of Dad's way of life. Mahwah was a local stop on the Erie railroad, and trains from there to New York would be few and slow. Suffern, some three miles away along the Franklin Turnpike (the road that paralleled the "Erie track") was an express stop, with more frequent and swifter trains to Jersey City, from which he would proceed to New York. The morning ritual Dad devised was a healthful walk to Suffern, daily Mass and Communion in the Church there, and the fastest transportation available to his work in New York.

2. There is controversy, locally, about the identity of the house described.

3. Here, in vivid description, is the course of the Erie local from Jersey City to Mahwah, whose eastward counterpart Dad avoided in the morning by walking to Suffern.

LETTERS

p. 153. 1. Dad's playful treatment of names is exercised here at his own expense, using the scorned "Alfred" in abbreviated form, and hyphenating his mother's name with his father's.

263

In the term "familee," he mocks the silent "e" found at the end of many names.

p. 154. 1. "Small Murray child" must be a playful reference to Aline Murray, older but smaller than Constance. "Sflager," as noted earlier, is Sarah Flagler Cary. Wortman is Denys Wortman, later successful as a comic artist. Viereck is George Sylvester Viereck, later known as a poet. Other names I have not identified.

p. 157. 1. "Mrs. Corbin," Sflager is here, in 1908, given her married name. "Ida" is unknown to me.
2. "Mrs. Payson," often mentioned, is unknown to me.

p. 158. 1. Mr. Bailey is George Bailey, mentioned in several letters. From the context, it is evident that he is an English editor.

p. 159. 1. Fiona Macleod, pseudonym of William Sharp.

p. 160. 1. "Our little Howard," unidentified.

p. 162. 1. "147" is 147 College Avenue, the residence in New Brunswick of Dr. and Mrs. Fred B. Kilmer.
2. "Seaumas O'Shiel." Either Dad or Granny's typist had as much trouble spelling Shaemas O'Sheel as I in my childhood.

p. 163. 1. "Harold," unidentified.

p. 166. 1. I don't know what operation I had.
2. Netty (or Nettie) was a long-time cook in the Kilmer house in New Brunswick.

p. 167. 1. "Glen Swigget" is Glen Levin Swiggett.
2. "Edith Thomas," is Edith Matilda Thomas, a poet, who usually wrote as Edith M. Thomas. Her *Selected Poems*, Harper, 1926, included a poetic tribute by Ada Alden, called "Psyche's Lamp."

p. 169. 1. "The Parkers": unknown to me.
2. Miss Molt. I don't remember her first name, but I remember the two sisters, Miss Molt and Mrs. Bignold (sp.?), who lived not far from the Kilmer College Avenue house in New Brunswick. When I was in New Brunswick, Christmas or other holidays, I often got to visit them and admire their large and elegantly furnished doll house.

p. 170. 1. Red Cross Notes. By an agreement with the American Red Cross, Johnson & Johnson has been allowed the use of the red cross symbol. Red Cross Notes was a Johnson & Johnson publication, for which Grandad, Dr. Fred B. Kilmer, was chiefly responsible.

264

p. 172. 1. McAlister *may* mean McAlister Coleman, Dad's close friend, I think classmate (Rutgers or Columbia), and my godfather. I don't know anything about Helen Hardenburgh.

p. 175. 1. Julia Marlow, a famous actress, is probably listed among the contributors to *Moods* as Dad's little joke.

p. 176. 1. Dad's project of translating "The Cherry Garden" was probably never completed.

p. 177. 1. The month, not named in this letter, is March. My actual birthday in 1910 was Monday, March 21, but of course the observance would take place on a Sunday, so that Dad could participate.
　　　 2. The minister, Elisha Brooks, is jokingly referred to as "Comrade" on account of Dad's adherence (at the time) to the Socialist Party.
　　　 3. "King" is Frederick Allen King, Dad's associate in various aspects of the Funk & Wagnalls work, and his successor as poetry editor of *The Literary Digest*.

p. 178. 1. "Glenzer" is Richard Butler Glaenzer, an editor and author.

p. 179. 1. "L____" is whoever was editor of the Sunday New York Times in 1909. Possibly Louis Wetmore?
　　　 2. "Old Mr. Yeats," may be fact or fiction. William Butler Yeats did sometimes visit New York—I have seen a photograph of him conversing with Grandaddy. Others listed are, spelled right and named fully, Eric Bell, David Snedden, Alfred Kreymborg, Alanson Hartpence, Van Wyck Brooks. Others, besides Mother and Dad, are Norman Poe and (Edward) Gordon Craig, active in many aspects of the theater, son of Ellen Terry and Edward Godwin.

p. 182. 1. Mollie Campbell. The Misses Campbell, two of them, were friends, and somehow related to us.
　　　 2. In calling Theodore Roosevelt "your friend," Dad is joking, as usual. His parents were too conservative to be fond of the "Bull Moose" Republican.

p. 183. 1. What lake and what mountain? Anyone's guess. The Albany relatives were probably kinfolk to Granny, since Annie Kilburn was born in Albany.
　　　 2. Mr. Pickering is unknown to me. Frank Vietelly was a long-time editor for Funk & Wagnalls in their various publications.
　　　 3. Reed's is presumably a bookstore in New Brunswick. *Summer of Love*, Dad's first book, was published by The Baker & Taylor Company.
　　　 4. Dugald Stewart Walker, author and artist, and Stuart Walker, playwright and producer, were friends and shared

an apartment. The fact that Dugald Walker was called "Stewart" didn't help in clarifying which was which. Dad's reference is *probably* to Dugald Stewart Walker, since it has to do with pictures.

p. 184. 1. Mrs. Trask is Katrina Trask (Mrs. Spencer Trask), playwright and novelist.

p. 185. 1. Le Gallienne is Richard Le Gallienne.
2. Russell Her<u>ts</u>, writer and editor, usually signed himself as B. Russell Herts.
3. Barrie (probably the same as "Barry," is unknown to me.

p. 186. 1. The Emily Grigsby reference is a mystery to me.

p. 187. 1. The great boulder in the front yard of the Mahwah house now bears a plaque to identify the place as formerly inhabited by Joyce Kilmer and family.
2. "Mr. Guy," evidently a clergyman, is unknown to me. I can't remember my comments.

p. 188. 1. William Wymark Jacobs, who wrote as W. W. Jacobs, was one of the favorite authors of my childhood. My much-read copy is inscribed, "To Joyce from Mother, Kilburn, Coxwold, Yorks. 25th July - 1911," the very copy of *The Skipper's Wooing* that is mentioned in this letter.
2. *The Black Tulip* is a novel by Alexandre Dumas père.
3. Conan Doyle needs no identification here.
4. Snaith is John Collis Snaith, usually identified as J. C. Snaith, an author of light novels.

p. 190. 1. Rosamonde is Rose Kilburn Kilmer. Dad enjoyed stretching names for the fun of it, sometimes satisfying himself by merely adding a silent "e." I was christened Kenton Sinclair Kilmer, but was amused, a few years ago, to note that my Morristown birth certificate named me, in Dad's handwriting, as Kenton Sinclair<u>e</u> Kilmer.
I wonder what Dad thought about Mother's two sisters, one of whom was married to Mr. Clark<u>e</u>, and the other to Captain Green<u>e</u>.

p. 194. 1. James Gray, long a family friend, was for many years Literary Editor of the *New York Sun*. Mac *may* be McAlister Coleman (mentioned on page 172 as McAlister), but other Macs are possible.

p. 196. 1. Ampl<u>e</u>forth Abbey is one of the principal Roman Catholic Benedictine monasteries in England. Gray is James Gray, mentioned on page 194.

p. 197. 1. The diarist is, of course, Samuel Pepys. I don't whether it was Dad or the transcriber who misplaced the apostrophe.

2. *The Heptalogia*, or Seven Against Sense, is a collection of seven parodies of noted English poets, by Algernon Charles Swinburne.

p. 202. 1. I'm not sure of the identify of the Pages.

p. 203. 1. I think the item that Dad thought would amuse his mother is a story *my* mother told me, of a tribute paid at the Board of Health dinner in New Brunswick to Grandad: "In times of public need, Dr. Kilmer has always been ready, and has most always done so!"

p. 204. 1. The digging of the blind drain is the operation described from my childish memory, on page 88.

p. 207. 1. "The Wiban Chanticleer" must be a transcriber's error. Dad certainly knew the word was "Urben"! Handwritten letter?

p. 209. 1. "Montagu" is probably Charles Edward Montague, British journalist, novelist, and critic.

p. 210. 1. "Dr. Farkashozy" is unidentified. The name seems improbable.

p. 212. 1. Leonard Abbot is Leonard Dalton Abbott.

p. 213. 1. "Sapphies" is meant to be Sapphics.

p. 214. 1. The reference to the "Dam family" reminds me of a much later occurrence. My wife and I, with our then eight children, were traveling by train to Canada, intending a vacation on Bonaventure Island. The conductor, looking us over, said: "Mr. and Mrs. Dam, I presume?" "Yes," I answered, "and we've brought the whole family."

p. 218. 1. Miss Cone is the poet, Helen Gray Cone.
2. Miss Widemer is Margaret Widdemer, poet and novelist.
3. Miss Klauser is unknown to me.

p. 222. 1. Albert Crockett is Albert Stevens Crockett, writer and publicist.

p. 223. 1. Miss Berg was a practitioner of "Swedish massage," using the technique to help Rose overcome the paralysis left after her bout of what is now called polio.

p. 224. 1. In what sense Epes Sargent was Granny's "old friend" is a mystery to me. This could be fact, or it could be a joke.

p. 225. 1. Mr. Smilter is unknown to me.

p. 226. 1. Mrs. Byer is unknown to me.

p. 227. 1. The commencement address in Winona, MN, was probably at St. Teresa's College, a college for girls.

p. 229. 1. Campion College, where Dad made many Jesuit friends, was a high school, in spite of its name. The Joyce Kilmer archive that was formed there has been transferred, since the closing of the school, to Marquette University, Milwaukee, Wisconsin.
2. Cliff Haven, New York, was the site of a Jesuit retreat house, which I believe is where Dad was planning the stay mentioned in this letter. P. 233 speaks of a summer school there.
3. Edward Marshall is unknown to me.
4. The book of Belloc's poems mentioned here is the American edition of his *Verses*.

p. 231. 1. Dad's stay in the Good Samaritan Hospital in Suffern, NY, was on account of broken ribs suffered when he crossed the tracks, hastily, just as his express train arrived to take him to New York. He had attended Mass and received Communion in the Suffern church, as was his custom, but was late in getting to the station, where there was no safe walkway across the tracks. I remember visiting him in the hospital, and seeing his chest all bound up in adhesive tape.

p. 232. 1. Mt. Graylock, a misspelling of Mount Greylock, in Massachusetts.

p. 235. 1. The bound volumes of Punch, and the volumes of Leech's drawing, mentioned here, are now in my library.

p. 236. 1. Fr. O'Connor is unknown to me.
2. The anthology, *Dreams and Images*, was published, not by Doran, but by Liveright. It was later issued as *Joyce Kilmer's Anthology of Catholic Poets*.

p. 237. 1. The address at Campion was published as "The Courage of Enlightenment."
2. The Alfred Watts poems were parodies of the *vers libre* of the period, particularly the "imagist" school. They were taken seriously by some little magazines of the time.
3. The Dr. Condon mention is about a murder case that puzzled authorities, and was still being brought up in the news in the twenties and thirties.
4. The specifically dated letter indicates a time in the summer of 1917 when Dad was still in the 7th Regiment.

p. 238. 1. These letters, from p. 238 through the first one on p. 240, were probably written prior to the one of July 10.
2. Miss Sillcocks is unknown to me.

p. 243. 1. The magazine that awarded the first and second prizes to Dad's poems was *The Queen's Work*.
2. The member of the wedding not mentioned in the description (other than the groom, Captain Stanley Greene) is the

ring bearer, Kenton. It was thought that the ring might fall off its cushion, so the best man had the wedding ring in a vest pocket, and Constance and Tad borrowed Gran's wedding ring and had it sewed onto the cushion. I was programmed to turn the cushion over at the moment at which the presiding minister asked for the ring, while the best man would produce the ceremonial ring from his pocket and hand it to Tad, the groom. This would have gone over without a hitch, except that Gran, in her place in front and on the aisle, reached out and sternly turned my cushion back, so that the ring was once again on top. My mother told me, later, that as I put the ring under, once again, I gave Gran a LOOK!

3. Gran was in dutch about the announcements, too. She had been in charge of getting them printed, and she had spelled Tad's name "Stanleigh" on the whole lot, and mailed them out before anyone could notice the strange spelling. She explained later that she had thought the name Stanley would look more elegant that way.

p. 243. 1. Camp Mills, in Mineola, Long Island, New York, was the only training camp at which I was able to visit Dad. I went there perhaps once, perhaps twice, with Mother.

p. 244. 1. I was the only one of the children who had whooping-cough. In September, 1917, Rose died (September 9) and Christopher was born (September 29). Rose was buried in the family plot in New Brunswick, and I was staying with Margaret Widdemer in her house on Shepherd Place in Larchmont. Deborah had to have her tonsils out in a New York hospital while Mother was in a "lying in hospital" for Christopher's birth. Michael was taken care of by Gran and Grandaddy in New York. While I was at the Widdemer house I somehow contracted whooping-cough, and I remember Mother's telling me with what horror she met me, on our reunion in Larchmont, she holding baby Christopher, and Deborah and Michael standing beside her, and I came up to them and gave a great whooping cough! She thought they might all catch it, but none did. I coughed so hard that I broke a blood vessel in one eye, and had to wear a black patch (like a pirate, I thought happily) for some weeks.

p. 246. 1. Dad's Council of the Knights of Columbus was the one in New Rochelle, whose meetings he had been able to get to from the nearby Larchmont house.

p. 247. 1. Maurice Kane is unknown to me.
2. *Monksbridge* is the book by John Ayscough, pseudonym of Monsignor Francis Browning Drew Bickerstaffe-Drew, an

English Roman Catholic clergyman and prolific author. I remember a tale my mother told about his visit to our house one time, when he was on a lecture tour through the United States with his nephew, Frank. At breakfast, he remarked about the family eating habits: "Eauw! Frank! They put *salt* on their *melon*! Eauw! Frank! They put *sugar* on their *porridge*!"

p. 249. 1. There are many Lakewoods, but I think I may guess confidently that Granny was holidaying in Lakewood, New Jersey.

       2. As I recall, that medal wasn't for over-all excellence, but just for arithmetic. It was the *tiniest* gold meal I have ever seen, but I was proud to be awarded it. I was just finishing third grade.

p. 254. 1. "Scruge-like" is probably meant to be "Scrooge-like," a likely terminology for Dickens enthusiasts like Dad and Granny. I have no idea what the elided identification was.

p. 258. 1. Eden Phillpotts, the English novelist and playwright, as meant here. I'm not sure of the correctness of the title, "Old Delaboll."

p. 259. 1. Emmett Watson was a highly talented illustrator. His painting of a tiger, a Saturday Evening Post cover in the early twenties, when I was in high school, was well remembered for decades. The illustration for "Rouge Bouquet" was used when the poem was printed in *Scribner's*. I met his son or grandson (sorry for the vagueness of my memory) at an observance in honor of Colonel Donovan at the CIA Headquarters. He had inherited a full-size wall painting of the "Rouge Bouquet" illustration, and was having to leave the building in which it was. I urged him to let the 69th Regiment know about it, and see if they couldn't arrange a way to get it into the Armory in New York.

       2. Mrs. Denis Eden was Helen Parry Eden, an Anglo-Irish essayist. She became my mother's friend by correspondence, and then mine.

p. 261. 1. Grandad's trouble, mentioned in this letter, was called a "nervous breakdown." It required hospital confinement for a period, I think of some months, and his recovery was complete.

INDEX

Abbott, Leonard Dalton...........194-195, 212
Academy, The 194-195
Acrostic on the Lusitania (AKK poem).....222
Adams, MA................................231, 233
Adirondacks.....................................254
Alarm Clock 185
Albany, NY 183
Alden, Ada (Gran)....1-2, 53, 54, 62, 72-73, 199
Alden, Henry Mills (Grandaddy) 1-2, 22,
                    25, 26, 39, 72, 155, 242
American Expeditionary Forces 244,
            246-247, 251, 253, 255, 257, 260
American Express 246
Ampleforth Abbey.............................196
Annunciation, The (JK poem) 242
Anthology of French Verse 187
Apple Blossoms (book)..........................26
Archbishop of York 259
Argosy, The......................................229
Arlington, VT 231, 232
Arliss, George 217
Armistice Day 1
Armstrong, Mary 3
Ashley, Raymond 154
Atheneum, The............................194-195
Auerbach, Berthold 52
Austen, General 241
Authors' Club.............................178, 199
Ayscough, John (pseudonym)................247
Bab Ballads (book) 54
Bailey, George 158-9, 161-162, 174
Baker & Taylor Co. 183, 199
Baldwin, Stephen Charles 192
Ballad of the Brave Wanton, The
        (JK poem) 190, 194-195
Ballade of Butterflies (JK poem)............168
Bally Pub, The (JK essay)....................234
Bang, The..169
Barrie (?)..185
Barry (?) 179
Bartender, The (JK poem) 216
Bass's Pale Ale...............................19, 77
Beer 19, 73, 77
Bell, Eric 179
Bellman, The 201, 205, 230
Belloc, Hilaire 37, 229
Bellows Pipe, MA...............................232
Berg, Miss......................................223
Berkshires 228, 232
Bickerstaffe-Drew, Msgr. Francis...........247
Black Tulip, The................................188
Blackbird and His Mate, A (To a Blackbird
        and His Mate who Died in the Spring,
        JK poem).....................................193
Blue Bird, The 182
Boni & Liveright 248

Book News Monthly 222, 226
Booklover, The (JK essay) 234-235
Bookman 225
Brat (JK term for his mother) 153
Brewer, William A. 4, 24
British Review, The............................203
Brook Farm Community 22
Brooke, Rupert 46, 218, 221
Brooks, Van Wyck 179
Browning, Robert...............................37
Buffalo, NY 220, 227
Burton Ale 231
Business as Usual................................256
Butler, Ellis Parker 227
Butterfly Ballade (JK poem) 179
Byers, Mrs. 226
Byrne, Brian Donn 105
California 252
Call for Mr. Keefe (Lardner story) 251
Call, The 178
Cambridgeshire 260
Camp Mills, Mineola, Garden City,
        Long Island 240, 243, 247
Campbell, Mollie 182
Campion College 229-230, 236-237
Canada 254
Canadian Pacific 210
Cap and Gown......................227, 229-230
Cape Cod, MA 228
Carbery, Ethna 106
Carlin, Francis...................................105
Cathedral of Rheims (poem)....................53
Catholic World, The 201, 203, 206
Cawein, Madison Julius.......................239
Century, The 244
Chanticleer 182
Chasse, Charles 170
Cherry Orchard, The 176
Cheshire, England 238
Chesterton, Gilbert Keith 195-196
Chevely Crossing (JK poem) 179
Chicago, IL 233
Child's Garden of Verses 38
Christmas 176
Christmas boxes 245
Church Times, The................194-195, 197
Churchman, The 198-199, 203
Circus...210
Circus and Other Essays
        (JK book) 226, 229
Circus, The (JK essay) 61-62, 221
Clarke, Ada Murray 2, 25
Cleveland, OH 230
Cliff Haven, NY....................229, 231-234
Coerr, Sarah (see Sflager)
Coleman, McAlister 172

Collins, Wilkie 245
Mary Colum...............................104-112
Colum, Padraic..................................104
Columbia Club....................................185
Columbia University.....................48, 199
Company K 240
Comstock School 217
Condon, Dr. 237
Cone, Helen Gray..............................218
Contemporary Scottish Verse 53
Copperhead, The (play) 252
Corbin, Sarah (see Sflager)
Corbins 173
Cosgrove's Ale 227-230
Coulevain, Pierre de...........................205
Courage of Enlightenment, The
    (JK address)................................237
Court Musicians (JK poem) 181
Cox, Eleanor Rogers 78, 109
Coxwold, Yorkshire.............................196
Cragmere (see Mahwah)
Craig, (Edward) Gordon
    ("Ellen Terry's son") 179
Crockett, Albert 222
Croix de Guerre 118
Current Literature.......................168, 199
Current Opinion.................................212
Curtis, George William 22
Daily Travelling (JK essay)..................221
Daly, T(homas) A(ugustine)..................112
Daly, Father James J. 108
Dave Lilly (JK poem) 4, 10, 75, 232
Dead Lover, The (poem)........................54
De la Mare, Walter 37
Delicatessen (JK poem) 207-208
Delta Upsilon Fraternity 154, 160
Delta Upsilon Fraternity House 48
Derbyshire...260
Devan, Dr. Arthur ..22-23, 171, 191, 232-233
Dickens Convention, Rochester.......211, 214
Dickens Fellowship (New York) 51, 199,
    202, 207-208, 214, 221, 227, 250, 255
Dickens Fellowship (Rochester).......211, 215
Dickens Fellowship, London...........211, 221
Dickens Land (book) 211
Dickens Pageant.................................208
Dickens, Charles 164, 168
Dictionary of the Thames.....................168
Dictionary, Funk & Wagnalls................183
Disgust...197
Divina Commedia 183
Dobson, Austin 54
Dodd, Mead & Co. 248
Dogwood tree.....................................200
Donnelly, Eleanor 112
Doran, George H. Co., The.............214, 236
Douglas, Sir George 53
Doyle, Sir Arthur Conan ...188, 209-210, 248
Dream Days 166

Dreams and Images (JK anthology) 229,
    236, 238, 241, 248, 251
Drill and guard duty 239-241, 243
Drivel Day..69
Dublin Review.......................193-195, 197
Duffy, Father Francis Patrick ..109, 119, 244
Dumas, Alexandre 188
Dupont, Aime (photographer)...............247
D'Youville College..............................220
Earls, Father Michael, SJ 112
East Wind (poem)................................26
Easter.......................................177, 218
Eastman, Charles Alexander 25
Eastman, Elaine Goodale.................25, 26
Eddy, Dave 232
Eden, Helen Parry (Mrs. Denis) 259
Edward VII 179, 185, 188
Edwin Drood 211
Eggplant 19
Eliot, George.......................................52
Ellery Queen's Mystery Magazine 20
England 18, 21, 247, 252, 256, 259
England, bombings............................220
Erie Railroad 62
"Evening Times" 208
Excelsior (poem) 54, 55
Eye Witness, The 193-198
Fairfax Family in Fairfax County 25
Fairfax, Va. 25
Farkashozy, Dr. 210
Farrish's Chop House, New York.....219, 225
Faure, Mme. 205
Favete Linguis (AK poem)......................60
Federation of Women's Clubs...............230
Ferris, Tom 208
Fighting Sixty-Ninth 118
Finley-Acker 247
First Congregational Church
    (Flushing, NY) 218
Flying Inn, The (book)...........................37
Folly (JK poem) 6, 214
Forum, The..185
France.......2, 8, 24, 48, 52, 66, 74, 103, 110,
    118, 119, 246-247, 253 255, 257, 259-261
From the Easy Chair (book)....................22
Funk & Wagnalls..21, 168, 171-174, 177, 178
Gale, N.Y. 18, 155-162
George Meredith (JK poem)..................166
George V 185, 188
George, Lloyd 197
Georgetown Preparatory School 23, 108
Georgetown University Library..........24, 54
Germany 198, 219
Gielgud, John.....................................20
Gift, The (poem) 56
Gifts of Shee 198
Gilbert, William Schwenk......................54
Gillilan, Strickland 37
Glaenzer, Richard Butler....................178

Gloucester, MA 224
Golden Age, The 166
Good Samaritan Hospital, Suffern (NY) ..231
Goodale, Dora Read 25, 26
Grahame, Kenneth 166
Gramercy Park 185
Gray, James 194, 196, 204
Greene, Captain Nathaniel 242
Greene, Constance Murray 2, 51, 72,
                                            199, 242
Greenes' Wedding 242
Grey Nuns of Montreal 220
Greystone 215
Grigsby, Emily 186
Grimsby, Ontario, Canada 227-230
Guiney, Louise Imogen 110
Guy, Mr. (?).....................................187
Gypsies 75
Hardenburgh, Helen 172
Hardy, Thomas 52
Harlow, Caroline Giltinan 103-104
Harper's Magazine.................2, 22, 25, 72
Harper's Weekly 22, 186, 206, 221, 225
Hartpence, Alanson............................179
Harvey, Alexander 169
Headquarters Company ...244, 246-247, 251,
                          253, 255, 257, 259-260
Healy's Golden Glades............236, 239, 242
Henri's 254, 261
Heptalogia, The 197, 204
Hertz, B. Russell 185
High Kilburn, Yorkshire......................161
High Tide on the Coast of Lincolnshire 37
Higher Education Association 172
Hinkson, Katherine Tynan 110
Holliday, Robert Cortes...........................5
Holmes, Sherlock...............................248
Homer......................................53, 58, 109
Hopkins, Father Gerard, S.J. 45
House and Garden 229
House With Nobody In It, The
    (JK poem) 39, 90-91, 225
Howitt, Mary 37
Hudson Tube 62, 173
Hughes, Charles Evans 235
Hull, England 222
Hunter College 218
Hussif (sewing kit) 237, 241
Ice Cream Cone 62
If I Were King...................................210
In Memory of Rupert Brooke
    (JK poem) 218, 221, 225
Indian Legends Retold (book)..................25
Ingelow, Jean 37
Insurance 252
Intelligence Section 253, 257, 260-261
International, The...................190, 194-195
Irish 103-113
Irish Whisky with syrup........................20

Jackson Whites 191
Jacob Ruppert's Knickerbocker Beer ..19, 77
Jacobs, William Wymark 188
Jeffries-Johnson fight 181
Jersey City Terminal 62
Jesus and the Summer Rain (JK poem)....178
Johnson & Johnson...........................163
Johnson, Lionel.................................220
Joyce Kilmer Forest 75
Kaiser, The.................................222-223
Kane, Maurice 247
Kelly, Blanche Mary 112
Kelly, Father John Bernard 109, 118
Kennerly, Mitchell 185
Kilburn family 153
Kilburn Hall, Yorkshire 257, 259
Kilmer, Aline Murray ("Mother")..........1-4,
    18-39, 42-43, 47-49, 51-62, 64, 72-74, 79-80,
        82-83, 87, 89, 97-98, 100-105, 107-112,
    118-119, 155, 158-159, 161, 163, 168-171,
    173, 177, 179, 183, 185-187, 190, 193-194,
    196, 198-199, 203, 206, 210-211, 218, 226,
                     229, 238, 248, 249, 251
Kilmer, Annie Kilburn ("Granny")...1, 3, 22,
                        24, 39, 51, 103, 205
Kilmer, Charles Henry 103
Kilmer, Christopher 2, 28, 108, 119,
                                      120, 238
Kilmer, Deborah.....2, 28, 31, 38, 69, 70, 108
                      218, 223, 233, 236, 238
Kilmer, Frances Frieseke............24, 52, 103
Kilmer, Frederick Barnett ("Grandad") 1,
    155-6, 158-159, 161-163, 165, 174-175, 178,
    180, 190, 198-199, 206-207, 213, 226-227,
    229, 238-239, 247-248, 251-252, 256, 261
Kilmer, Joyce (Dad) 1-23, 25, 37-42,
    44-46, 48-54, 57-78, 81-92, 94-99, 103-129
Kilmer, Kenton (Puff) 166, 168-178, 174,
    178, 180, 182-183, 185-188, 190, 193-194,
    196-199, 210-211, 214, 218, 220, 232, 234,
                                 238, 249
Kilmer, Michael Barry 236, 238
Kilmer, Miriam 37
Kilmer, Rosamonde, see Kilmer, Rose Kilburn
Kilmer, Rose Kilburn..........2, 190, 193-194,
    196-199, 201, 204, 211, 214, 218, 223,
                           233-234, 238
King, Frederick Allen....................184-185
King's Ballade (JK poem)....................179
Klauser, Miss 218
Knights of Columbus 246
Kreymborg, Alfred............................179
L---(Wetmore, Louis?)........................179
Lake Champlain 229
Lake Isle of Innisfree, The 189
Lake View House, Gale, NY 155-160
Lakewood, NJ (?) 249, 252, 255
Larchmont, NY 236, 260
Lardner, Ring 251

Leamy, Edmund 110
Leamy, Margaret 109, 110
Lecture tour by JK 225-226
Leech, John.....................................235
LeGallienne, Richard........................185
Leslie, Shane 187
Lewissohn, Ludwig 167
Liberal Party (England) 213
Library of Congress 22, 23, 104
Life on the ocean wave, A.....................224
Lippincott's Magazine 223
Literary Digest, The....21, 170, 172, 186, 199
Literature in the Making (JK interviews)..229
Little Town of Bethlehem, The (play) 184
Lizette (JK poem) 161
London 202-203, 223, 233
Long Island Sound 236
Longfellow, Henry Wadsworth 37, 55
Love's Rosary (JK poem) 180
Love's Thoroughfare (JK poem) 180
Lusitania, The 222, 224
MacKaye, Percy 175
Macleod, Fiona (William Sharp) 53, 159
MacManus, Seumas 106
Madelon (song) 258-259
Madison Square Garden 61
Madness (JK poem) 54, 186
Maeterlinck, Maurice........................159
Mahwah, NJ.........21, 49, 55, 61, 62, 64, 72,
     75-77, 87-89, 95, 97, 109, 189-192, 194,
                200, 203, 210, 226, 231
Mail 251, 253
Main Street (JK poem) 229
Main Street and Other Poems
     (JK book)......................229, 236, 242
Man with the Hole, The 168
Manalive 195-196
Map of England 210-211
Markham, Edwin...............................168
Marlowe, Julia 175
Marshall, Edward 229
Martin (JK poem) 14, 15, 54, 192
Martin Chuzzlewit...........................51, 192
Masefield, John.................................239
Mass 74, 97, 107
Maynard, Theodore 37, 104, 112
McCarthy, Denis A..........................105, 106
McCarthy, Justin Huntley....................210
Measles 185
Meatless, wheatless days 250, 255, 257
Meerschaum pipe 191, 201
Memorial Day (JK poem) 203
Memories of My Son (AKK book).............51
Meredith, George 52, 170
Metamorphosis (JK poem) 54
Metuchen, NJ 23-26, 39, 154, 168, 182
Mexico 207, 232
"Miss Joyce Kilmer" 208
Mississippi River 233

Molt, Miss 169
Monksbridge 247
Montague, Charles Edward......209, 212, 217
Montreal, Quebec, Canada...................229
Moods 165, 167, 170, 175
Moods Publishing Co. 176
Moody, William Vaughn......................239
Moriarty, Helen L. 112
Moroso, John A..........................177, 180
Morristown High School 170, 172
Morristown, NJ.....19, 23, 159, 162, 164, 166
Mother Goose 38
Mount Greylock, MA....................232-233
Mount Houvenkopf, NJ.................191, 211
Mount Houvenkopf (JK poem) 211
Mountain Dooryards............................26
Moustache 228, 230
Murray, Ada Foster (see Alden, Ada)
Murray, Aline (see Kilmer, Aline)
Murray, Constance (see Greene, Constance
     Murray)
Murray, Kenton C................................1
Mustard 19, 21, 62
Naiads (JK poem) 163
Nation, The (New York) 188, 218
National Arts club.............................242
Netherton, Nan.................................26
Nettie (or Netty).............................3, 166
Netty (see Nettie)
New Age, The 182, 195
New Brunswick Home News 165, 205
New Brunswick, NJ........2, 3, 18, 23, 24, 51,
     77, 162, 164-165, 169, 171, 173, 176-177,
     178, 180-181, 182-183, 188, 197, 203, 227,
                230, 235, 237
New Witness (London) 218, 219, 259
New York, NY 21, 23-24, 38, 51, 61, 62,
     70, 72, 75, 97, 168, 171-174, 176, 182, 187,
          227-228, 233, 235, 237, 240, 242
New York Times, The......190, 199, 206, 211,
               213-214, 224, 239-240
New York Times Book Review, The 198,
               201, 204-205
New York Times Sunday Magazine 203
Nicholas Nickleby 165, 202
Nickleby, Mrs. 208
Nine Bean Rows 189
Noyes, Alfred...................................206
O'Bryan, Sadie (Mrs. Frieseke).......103, 112
Ocean Beach, NY 24
O'Connor, Father 236
O'Donnell, Father Charles L.CSC..........106
Ohiyesa (C.A. Eastman).......................25
Old Delaboll (Phillpotts book)..............258
Old Poets (JK poem)...........................215
Omar the Tentmaker (play) 211
One Hundred and Sixty-fifth Regiment,
     US Infantry 240, 244, 246-247, 249,
          251, 253, 255, 257, 259-260

Opera House Drug Store 23
Oppenheim, James 168
O'Sheel, Shaemas 44, 110, 111, 162,
175, 180, 186
Our Island Saints 38
Oxford 191
Oxford and Cambridge Review, The 197
Oxfordshire....................................259
Park Avenue Hotel............................235
Parker, Father................................204
Pathfinder, The........167, 170, 175, 184, 188
Paul Revere's Ride 37
Paul Robeson High School 3
Peacemaker, The 259
Peacock Pie 37
Pennies (JK poem)........................192-193
Pepys' Diary 197, 204
Pepys, Samuel 197
Person of the House, The.....................197
Philadelphia, PA 178
Phillpotts, Eden 258ᶠ
Photographs 250, 254-255, 257, 260-261
Physical examination 241
Pickering, Mr. 183
Pied Piper of Hamelin 37
Pittsfield, MA 238
Plattsburg, NY (training camp) 232
Poe, Norman 179
Poetry prize medal............................237
Poetry Society of America 199, 215, 237
Poetry: a Magazine of Verse.................200
Polish Blood 54
Post (New York?)..............................165
Post, New York 187
Postage stamps................................238
Pound, Ezra 185
Prairie du Chien, WI..229-230, 233, 236, 238
Prayer to Bragi (JK poem).............167, 170
Prior, Matthew 53
Professor Jackson 48
Prohibition 220, 259
Protestant Episcopal Church 202
Proud Poet, The (JK poem)............44, 230
Public Opinion (London) 216
Puff (see also Kilmer, Kenton) 21
Punch...........................197, 219, 234-235
Ramapos 231
Raspberries...................................18, 161
Reader's Encyclopedia 22
Reading 37-38, 52-53, 73, 75, 87-88
Rector's 261
Red Cross Notes...................163, 165, 170
Reedy, William Marion......................217
Regimental Intelligence Section 249
Robeson, Paul 3
Rogers Peet 237, 240-241
Roofs (JK poem)...........................17, 39
Roosevelt, Theodore 182, 193, 235
Rose and Grey (JK poem) 169

Rosenkavalier....................................187
Rouge Bouquet (JK poem)...................259
Rubaiyat stanzas (JK translation)....208, 211
Rutgers Preparatory School...................23
Rutgers University 154
St. Alexis (JK poem) 205
St. Louis Mirror 217
Sairey Gamp 51
Salads 19
Samaurai Press, The 185
San Francisco, CA 211, 248
Sapphics.......................................213
Sappho 213
Sargent, Epes 224
Saturday Evening Post.................251, 253
Savoy Hotel...................................235
Sceva, Eleanor Kilmer 1
Scollard, Clinton 167
Scott, Sir Walter 52, 216
Scouting 209
Scribner's..................................244, 259
Scribner's Book Store 172
Sentimental Journey, The 162
Sergeant....................................249, 253
Sergeant-Major 254
Servant Girl and Grocer's Boy
(JK poem) 200
Seventh Regiment Armory ..237-238, 240-242
Seventh Regiment, NY..........237, 239, 243,
246, 257
Sflager (also mentioned as Cary, Sarah
Flagler; Corbin, Sarah; and
Coerr, Sarah) 2, 23-25, 154, 156,
168, 173, 182, 244, 237-238, 240-242
Sharp, William (Fiona Macleod)..............53
Shields, James (see O'Sheel, Shaemas)
Shyne, Father Cornelius A. SJ.........108-109
Signs and Symbols (JK essay)................225
Sillcocks, Mrs. 238
Simpson (?) 178
Sinsinawa, WI 228-229
Sixty-ninth Regiment, NY........240, 243, 249
Skipper's Wooing, The 188
Smart Set, The........162, 165, 200-202, 205,
207-209, 214, 216
Smart Set Anthology 20
Smart Styles.............................207-208
Smith, Ellen 103
Smith, Hulda Curtis 22, 103
Snaith, John Collins 188
Snedden, David...............................179
Socialist Party 164, 175
Some Mischief Still (JK play) 209, 216
South Carolina...............................237
Southey, Robert................................37
Spanish-American War 108, 224
Spartanburg, SC (training camp).........235,
241, 243
Spectator, The (London)....182, 194-197, 216

Spider and the Fly, The 37
Standard, The 208
Stars (JK poem).....................202-203, 206
Statler Hotels 227, 233
Stephens, James 108
Sterne, Laurence..........................161-162
Strahan, Father Speer CSC 112
Stratford-on-Avon 217
Strauss, Richard 187
Strawberry icecream sodaless day 255
Suffern, NY 90-91, 95, 231
Suffragette, The 203
Suffragettes...................................213
"Suicide poem" (To a Young Poet
   Who Killed Himself) 202
Summer of Love (JK book) 54, 188
Sun, New York 166-167, 172
Sur la Branche..................................205
Sussex (torpedoed steamship) 229
Sweater...................................249, 251
Swiggett, Glen Levin 167
Swinburne, Algernon Charles 197
Sydney Carton....................................51
Symons, Arthur..................................188
Tale of Two Cities, A 51
Tales of the Mermaid Tavern 206
Terre d'Amour:..................................186
Terry, Ellen (see Craig)
This Is My America 4, 5, 24-26
Thomas, Edith Matilda 167
Thompson, Charles Willis 177
Thompson, Francis 239
Times Building 207
Timson & Co., John 246, 252
To Certain Poets (JK poem)...................205
To My Mother (JK poem) 216
Town and Country 165, 168
Transfer to 69th Regiment 240, 243
Trask, Katrina (Mrs. Spencer) 184
Treasure Island (play)..........................226
Trees (JK poem) 3, 74-77, 88, 89,
            92, 106, 200, 209, 214-215, 217
Trees and Other Poems (JK book).........205,
                                   214, 220
Tribute (JK poem)..............................170
Try a Tin Today (JK story) 224, 229
Tynan, Katherine (Hinkson)................110
Under Canvas (JK poem)....................223
Underwood & Underwood 217, 221
Untermeyer, Mrs. Samuel 215
Urban Chanticleer, The (JK essay) ...207-208
"Valentine" song................................214
Van Dyke, Henry 167
Van Noppen, Leonard Charles 168
Vaughn and Gomme (publishers) 216
Verhaeren, Emile 53
Verses, by Hilaire Belloc (JK preface) 229
Viereck, George Sylvester 154, 168, 175
Visitation, The (JK poem) 242

Vizetelly, Frank Horace 183, 226
Walker, Stewart 183
Walsh, Thomas 107, 116
War Mother (AKK poem).....................255
Warner's Library of the World's Best
   Literature (JK contributions) 239
Washington Post, The 4, 24, 68
Watson, Emmett 259
Watts, Alfred 237
Waverly (JK poem)............................216
Wells, Carolyn 112
Wetmore, Louis 179, 234, 239
White Ships and the Red, The
   (JK poem) 218, 224
Whitemail (JK story)............................20
Whooping Cough 244
Widdemer, Margaret.........109, 218-219, 237
Wilson, Woodrow...............................224
Wind in the Willows, The.....................166
Wine 20, 37
Winona, MN.............................227, 229
World I Saw, The 37
World War I 224, 226
Wortman, Denys..................................154
Wreck of the Hesperus, The...................37
Wright, Richardson............................191
Wupperman, Carlos.............................48
Y.M.C.A.................................244, 247
Yeats, William Butler...................179, 189
Yellow Gown, The (AKK song) 211
Yorkshire.................................212-213
Yorkshire Herald...............................204
Younger Choir, The....................168, 185

INDEX OF POEMS

Page

By ALINE KILMER

After Grieving 35
Against the Wall 29
Atonement 34
Candles That Burn 32
Experience..31
Favete Linguis 60
For the Birthday of a Middle-Aged Child 30
Gift, The 56
I Shall Not Be Afraid...36
If I Had Loved You More 102
Moonlight 47
My Mirror 27
One Shall Be Taken and the Other Left......................................101
Poor King's Daughter, The 80
Ptolemaic 59
Sanctuary 100
Song..43
Tribute
Vigils 79
Wind in the Night, A 33

By CHRISTOPHER KILMER

To Cornelius 108

By JOYCE KILMER

Apology (For Eleanor Rogers Cox) (Excerpt)..................................78
As Winds That Blow Against a Star (For Aline) 42
Blue Valentine, The...82
Citizen of the World 81
Dave Lilly..10
Delicatessen...7
Easter..86
Father Gerard Hopkins, S.J..45
Folly..6
Fourth Shepherd, The (For Thomas Walsh)...................................116
Gates and Doors 114
House With Nobody In It, The 90
In Memory of Rupert Brooke 46
In Memory 40
Kings 124
Love's Lantern (For Aline)..57
Main Street 71
Martin 14
Memorial Day 129
Peacemaker, The 127
Pennies...63
Prayer of a Soldier 128
Proud Poet, The (For Shaemas O'Sheel) (Excerpt) 44
Roofs...17
Rosary, The 99
Roses...84
Rouge Bouquet...125
Servant Girl and Grocer's Boy 16
Singing Girl, The 85
Snowman in the Yard, The (For Thomas Augustine Daly) 66
St. Alexis, Patron of Beggars 12
To a Blackbird and His Mate Who Died in the Spring 87
To a Young Poet Who Killed Himself 50
Trees (For Mrs. Henry Mills Alden)..92
Twelve-Forty-Five, The..94
Vision (For Aline) 58
White Ships and the Red, The 121

By KENTON KILMER

Shadows and Light...93

JOYCE KILMER
RUTGERS PREPARATORY SCHOOL, CLASS OF 1904

SERGEANT JOYCE KILMER, 1918

The state of North Carolina was chosen for a native American virgin forest, 3,800 acres named *The Joyce Kilmer Memorial Forest*. President Franklin D. Roosevelt sent a letter which stated, "It is particularly fitting that a poet who will always be remembered for the tribute he embodied in 'Trees' should find this living monument."

–July 30, 1936

"The world is the poorer for the loss of a very gallant gentleman and a poet who never wrote a line that was not pure, and sweet, and clean."

–Literary Digest, 1918

B-KIL
Kilmer, Kenton.
Memories of my father, Joyce
Kilmer.